Efficiency in U.S.
Manufacturing Industries

Efficiency in U.S. Manufacturing Industries

Richard E. Caves and
David R. Barton

The MIT Press
Cambridge, Massachusetts
London, England

This book was set in Palatino by Asco Trade Typesetting Ltd, Hong Kong and printed and bound by Halliday Lithograph in the United States of America.

Library of Congress Cataloging-in-Publication Data

Caves, Richard E.
  Efficiency in U.S. manufacturing industries / Richard E. Caves, David R. Barton.

    p.   cm.
  Includes bibliographical references.
  ISBN 0-262-03157-4
  1. United States—Manufactures—Labor productivity. 2. Industrial productivity—United States. I. Barton, David R. II. Title.
  HD9725.C38   1990
  338'.06'0973—dc20   89-28832
                                                                 CIP

Contents

Preface

Quantitative research in industrial organization has suffered a recession in recent years. The traditional mode of cross-section research fell under two clouds. First, it was not well suited for implementing empirically the deluge of new models of strategic behavior. (One might well ask whether any systematic empirical research technique is effective for that purpose.) Second, it ran through the obvious possibilities of testing the relation of allocative efficiency to the determining elements of market structure and performance. But this clouded status is undeserved. Many markets do embrace large numbers of participants, so that strategic behavior is of only passing significance. Furthermore, cross-section research techniques are generally valuable for identifying the structural determinants of market equilibria. Allocative efficiency (the incidence of "monopolistic distortions") is not the only normatively significant dimension of the allocation of resources.

In this book we report a substantial investigation of another normatively important dimension of resource use—technical or productive efficiency. This is a primitive aspect of economic efficiency, potentially of great importance but never a favorite of economists because of its resistance to analysis on the basis of traditionally preferred assumptions about economic behavior. We seek to combine recent developments in statistical methodologies and theoretical approaches to productive efficiency for a broad empirical investigation of the efficiency of U.S. manufacturing industries.

The project was begun in 1982 with the support of the Bureau of Industrial Economics, U.S. Department of Commerce. We are deeply grateful to the late Dr. Beatrice N. Vaccara for her help and encouragement. Other officials of the Department of Commerce who have offered assistance and encouragement over the years include

Frederick T. Knickerbocker, Kenneth M. Brown, and William B. Sullivan. The computations that underlie the project were supervised by Jay Waite and executed by Cyr Linonis at the U.S. Bureau of the Census. Additional assistance in organizing data used in chapters 6 through 8 was supplied by the Project for Industry and Company Analysis, supported by the Division of Research, Graduate School of Business Administration, Harvard University. Others who have contributed to the project include Zvi Griliches, C. M. Harris, Adam B. Jaffe, David G. Mayes, Derek J. Morris, S. J. Prais, F. M. Scherer, Alan Siu, Akio Torii, and Masu Uekusa. We received useful suggestions from seminar audiences at Harvard, Columbia, and the University of Connecticut. The opinions expressed are our own and not necessarily those of our employing institutions.

Efficiency in U.S. Manufacturing Industries

1   Introduction

Microeconomic analysis deals with efficiency in two senses: allocative efficiency, obtained by the best allotment of scarce resources among alternative activities and uses, and technical efficiency, achieved by minimizing the cost incurred to carry on each activity at any given level. The familiar marginal conditions for allocative efficiency are a central preoccupation of microeconomics in general and the study of industrial organization in particular. Technical efficiency, by contrast, has received little attention in economic research. The study reported here represents a broadly based effort to measure the technical efficiency of U.S. manufacturing industries and to explain why it varies among them.

Technical efficiency is "efficiency" in the popular sense of the word. Those untrained in economics frequently assume that it is a central concern of economists. Indeed economists commonly acknowledge that the gains they expect from improving the allocative efficiency of some activity or sector amount to only a smidgen of economic welfare—a smidgen relative to the gain from shaving a few percentage points off its unit costs (that is, raising its efficiency). Why technical efficiency receives so little attention is a matter of no small interest. Part of the answer lies in underdevelopment of the relevant theory. Indeed some economists declare technical efficiency to lie outside the reach of analytically founded economic analysis because the manager of an inefficient activity is failing to maximize its profits, and the maximization of profits by the business is taken as equivalent to the maximization of utility by the individual, a largely unquestioned axiom of economic analysis.

Given this touchstone of professional belief, it is paradoxical that, upon inspection, data on the distributions of cost and efficiency levels within industries regularly reveal what seem to be striking amounts of technical inefficiency. Klotz, Madoo, and Hanson (1981, p. 243) obtained from the 1967 Census of Manufactures data on the dispersions of plants' productivity levels in 102 U.S. manufacturing industries. In no industry was productivity (value-added per man-hour) in the top quartile of plants less than 25 percent greater than the industry-wide average. In the typical industry it was 65 percent greater, and in 16 industries it was more than double the average. Other times and places have yielded similar patterns. Flux (1913) called attention to the dispersion of net output per employee in data of the 1907 U.K. Census of Production and provided an astute list of factors that might contribute to explaining it.[1] Hazledine (1984) generated tabulations for Canadian manufacturing industries similar to those of Klotz, Madoo, and Hanson, finding that the price-cost margin in the higher-margin half of the average industry's plants was more than double the average margin in its low-margin half. Although these divergences are dramatic, they gained less attention than Leibenstein's (1966) reflection on consulting reports that showed the possibility of large productivity gains within plants or firms without adopting new technologies and simply by means of configuring existing inputs more efficiently. Leibenstein contributed the name *X-inefficiency* to what is called technical inefficiency in this study.[2]

More popular and immediate concerns also give forceful support to the study of technical efficiency. The once-supreme U.S. level of productivity in manufacturing industries was first threatened by more rapid rates of productivity growth in Japan and many European countries; then U.S. productivity levels came to be matched and exceeded at the same time the superior quality and/or more innovative designs of some foreign manufactures became widely evident. In short, an increasing fraction of U.S. manufacturing industry could be seen as technically inefficient relative to best practice abroad. Found among the orgy of diagnosis generated by this development are many propositions implying technical inefficiency within U.S. industries. For example, Hayes and Wheelright (1984, p. 20) charged that

there appears to have been a tacit agreement between firms in a number of important U.S. manufacturing industries over the past 15–20 years to compete primarily on dimensions other than manufacturing ability. . . . Therefore, attention and resources have been directed toward mass distribution, packaging, advertising, and the development of incremental new products to round out existing product lines or to attack specific market segments, instead of toward improving manufacturing capabilities.

The determinants of technical inefficiency within U.S. manufacturing industries can hardly avoid shedding light on popular hypotheses about gaps between average levels of productivity at home and abroad.

Our research rests on three foundation elements—a recently developed statistical technique for measuring technical efficiency, modern developments in economic analysis that generate cogent hypotheses about why and where it can exist, and the research methodology of testing determinants of performance on cross sections of industries, a well-proved technique in the field of industrial organization. The following sections briefly describe those foundation stones and explain the organization of the study.

1.1 Measurement of Technical Efficiency

The observer can determine the efficiency of a production unit, or the amount of inefficiency in the member units of an industry, only with the aid of some standard of optimal efficiency. Economic analysis rests on the assumption that a well-defined and generally known production function exists for each activity. Farrell (1957) first made operational the measurement of efficiency and characterized the ways in which a production unit can be inefficient. It can be technically inefficient by obtaining less than the maximum output available from whatever bundle of inputs it has chosen to employ. It can be allocatively inefficient by purchasing what is not the best bundle of inputs, given the prices of the various inputs and their marginal productivities in its production process.

Farrell's method was first put to use by means of linear-programming techniques, which infer the best-practice production function from the reported input-output combinations of some small number of the most efficient units. That method makes severe demands on the accuracy of the data (for those units that define the frontier) that are especially unwelcome in light of the wide dispersions noted in actual census tabulations—which presumably attain about as much accuracy as the outside researcher can hope for.

This stringent need for accurate data was relaxed by the development of the stochastic frontier production function, which assumes that the error term in a statistically fitted production function is composed of two components. One is the conventional (symmetrical) normal distribution of random elements, embracing errors in measurement, minor omitted variables, and the like. The other component is a one-sided distribution of amounts of technical inefficiency, its elements indicating shortfalls of the industry's production units from the efficient frontier. Technical inefficiency is assumed to reveal itself in the skewness of the (composed) residuals around a fitted production function, and only an assumption about the form of the distribution of technical-inefficiency levels is needed to extract an estimate of the average inefficiency of an industry's units.

The stochastic frontier production function has undergone a good deal of conceptual development and has seen many trial applications to particular data sets. In chapter 2 we review this literature, concluding that a simple version of the methodology holds promise for application across the board to U.S. manufacturing industries.

An arrangement was worked out whereby the U.S. Bureau of the Census would estimate frontier production functions for as many as possible of the four-digit manufacturing industries identified in the Standard Industrial Classification (SIC), using the Annual Survey of Manufactures plant panel's responses for the year 1977. Because the budget constraint precluded preliminary estimations with the whole set of industries, we selected a panel of twelve industries to test alternative specifications of the production function, measurements of key inputs, data-editing rules, and other tactical choices that might affect the results. This exploratory procedure and the consequent decisions are reported in chapter 3.

We obtained the frontier production functions, which yielded specific estimates of the amounts of inefficiency in a maximum of 347 industries. Several measures of inefficiency were calculated and their distributions analyzed for general plausibility and consistency with theory and relevant evidence. Our general conclusion—that the estimates (despite some problems) satisfy appropriate tests for credibility—is set forth in chapter 4.

1.2 Explaining Technical Efficiency: Theoretical Tools

Economic analysis has advanced greatly in its ability to treat failures in both organizations and markets that permit and sustain technical inefficiency. The first line of progress provides increasingly cogent answers to the question why technical inefficiency can exist, given the assumed unwillingness of citizens to leave currency on the footpath. If costs are elevated X percent above the minimum attainable, we must suppose that it pays somebody to reduce them. A satisfactory theoretical story must explain why that opportunity is not seized. The main part of the answer lies in second-best bargains struck between principals and agents—whether the owners of equity shares in firms and their hired managers or managers at any level within the enterprise and the persons whom they hire and supervise. The potential for second-best outcomes of such bargains and the implied strong possibility that the degree of nonoptimality will vary from case to case supply one basis for explaining technical efficiency.

This core approach can be embellished in various ways. Research embodying evolutionary and behavioral approaches to business organizations posits large fixed costs of renegotiating contractual arrangements among the agents who cooperate in the ongoing enterprise. Alternatively the hypothesis of utility maximization by individuals can be recast to allow for inert areas of behavior, such that better ways of doing things are sought actively only when satisfactory returns from current practice and the viability of present organizational arrangements become threatened. In chapter 5 we embody these propositions in some specific hypotheses about differences in industries' technical efficiency that should be associated with their differing structural characteristics.

The chapter also presents hypotheses flowing from contractual or organizational failures of a different kind. Another area of recent advance in economic analysis has been models of oligopolistic behavior. In particular, the sustainability of collusion has been closely examined, yielding new insight into why rivals may cooperate despite the fundamental inhibitor of the prisoners' dilemma. These theoretical advances join an older line of empirical research on industrial organization, which has unearthed much evidence that the ability of oligopolistic rivals to cooperate may differ among their market decision variables. Specifically cooperation to avoid price competition seems easier than avoiding noncooperative outcomes and preemptive moves in advertising and other sales promotion, product design and innovation, enlargements of plant capacity, and the like. Furthermore, cooperation on price affects the noncooperative choices that rivals make in other decision variables, with the implication that costs are not minimized for the bundle of goods and services (that is, including buyer information, product variety, innovation, auxiliary services) that an industry produces.

The essential defect of such an imperfect bargain within the oligopolistic industry is that rent seeking leads to inflation of some types of outlay beyond their socially optimal level (and perhaps deficient levels of other outlays). As a first approximation, we expect that such distortions would be indulged equally by all members of a group of symmetrical oligopolists. However, only weak assumptions about the irreversibility of some noncooperative moves and/or the randomness of their effects are needed to imply enlarged technical inefficiency—that is, an increased dispersion of competitors' apparent efficiency levels below what in this case is a revenue-productivity frontier.

In chapter 5 we propose a number of hypothesis of the form that technical efficiency decreases with the industry's structural opportunities for such degenerate oligopolistic bargains.

Hypotheses about technical inefficiency devolving from nonoptimal but persistent (quasi-)contractual arrangements within the firm or within the industry all have at least latent normative implications—although most economists despair of obtaining clear conclusions for public policy. The roster of hypotheses about technical efficiency developed in chapter 5 includes in addition many without any prima facie normative implication. That is, technical efficiency as we measure it picks up sources of differences in plants' or firms' productivity levels that involve no presumptive market failures. Important examples are product differentiation, spatial fragmentation of the market, and capital vintages that exhibit diverse productivity levels. They need to be controlled in order to complete the statistical model. However, knowledge of their impact and importance is substantively valuable for the message it conveys to business practitioners and others about sources of difference in the values of the opportunities that a market offers to different participants, and the potential payout of efforts to ensure that particular decisions are got right.

1.3 Interindustry Statistical Tests

The research methodology for testing these hypotheses is one traditional in industrial organization—cross-sections of industries at one point in time. In chapter 6 we use this method to test the hypotheses developed in chapter 5. An interindustry approach is not the only way to test hypotheses about technical efficiency, but it has much to contribute.[3] With minor exceptions, our hypotheses about technical efficiency treat it as a consequence of the structural opportunities inherent in a market and a phenomenon that settles down at a long-run equilibrium level. If many of its determinants are industry specific (but not specific to particular plants or firms), the industry becomes the presumptive unit of observation. Interindustry differences in technical efficiency lay reasonable claim to represent the long-run consequences of interindustry differences in stable elements of markets' structures. In principle these hypotheses could also be tested on changes over time in industries' structural elements and efficiency levels; however, this strategy provides little leverage in practice because few industries typically experience much change in most important elements of their structures.[4]

Very little precedent exists for the type of cross-section test devised and performed in chapters 5 and 6, although previous efforts by Downie (1958) and Carlsson (1972) are encouraging. In fact, the null hypothesis was rejected for many hypotheses advanced in chapter 5. These include hypotheses with important normative implications: import competition seems particularly salutary for enforcing efficiency, and corporate diversification is seriously hostile to it. By implication, these findings not only support important hypotheses but also validate the stochastic frontier production function methodology. This validation is a happy outcome in light of the methodology's weakness (uncovered in chapter 4) for establishing the average level of technical efficiency.[5] Accordingly we give no emphasis to the average extent of inefficiency implied by our findings, but the regression analysis of chapter 6 does attempt to quantify the gains available from changing various determinants of inefficiency.

Encouraged by the outcome of the interindustry test (chapter 6), we proceeded with two other analyses of technical efficiency suggested by the results. For more than 200 industries with relatively large numbers of plants, separate stochastic frontier production functions were estimated for the larger and smaller halves of plants in the Census Bureau's data base. From these functions we could determine whether efficiency bears any relation to plant (and thus company) size and test hypotheses about why such differences might exist.

That the dispersion of efficiency levels might decrease with the absolute sizes of plants (firms) is suggested by several factors, all consistent with past empirical research showing that the variance of firms' profit rates decreases with their sizes. Indeed the larger halves of a plants in the sampled industries prove on average more efficient than the smaller halves. While these intraindustry differences cannot be explained very well statistically, we did confirm several substantial hypotheses. Consider, for example, the finding from chapter 6 that enterprise diversification is hostile to efficiency. Diversified firms are the larger ones, and they tend to control the larger plants in an industry. Therefore, if the inefficient plants are indeed those supervised by managers distracted by their multi-industry commitments, the relative efficiency of large plants should decrease with the industry's involvement in enterprise diversification. That hypothesis is confirmed in the results reported in chapter 7.

With the success of the technical-efficiency measure established and many of its determinants apparently identified, we considered the testable consequences of technical efficiency. One of these, suggested by the organizational and evolutionary approaches to the theory of the firm, is that static inefficiency in the production unit might correspond to an inability to seize new opportunities and thus to attain productivity growth. It was attractive to pursue such an implication because these unconventional theoretical approaches are consistent with most of the hypotheses tested in chapter 6 but not necessary for them and thus are neither confirmed nor rejected by our findings about the determinants of static technical efficiency.

If an inefficient firm is hobbled for attaining productivity growth, does the industry's growth potential increase with the average efficiency of its member firms? Some problems of aggregation arise, but they do not appear to preclude testing the hypothesis at the industry level. Accordingly we investigated whether a simple measure of productivity growth from 1977 to 1986 increases with the levels of technical efficiency that industries exhibited in 1977. After controlling for productivity-growth opportunities, we found this hypothesis confirmed statistically. We also found the efficiency-increasing effects of import competition to have a strong counterpart in effects on productivity growth: changes in imports' market shares are positively associated (subject to long lags) with its rate of productivity growth. These results are reported in chapter 8.

The book concludes with reflections on this study's implications for public policy, business behavior, and future research (chapter 9). Fuller summaries of the empirical results can be found at the ends of chapters 4, 6, 7, and 8.

2   The Measurement of Technical Inefficiency

Research in the field of econometrics has made great progress in the last decade with methods for estimating the extent of technical inefficiency in a population of competing firms or plants. This chapter explores the definition and measurement of technical inefficiency and the research methods available for estimating it. Previous empirical applications of these methods and the substantive conclusions reached are reviewed briefly. The procedure employed in this project is then set forth.

2.1 Definition and Measurement of Technical Inefficiency

Because of the predominant concern of economics with allocative efficiency, only in the last three decades has attention been paid to the measurement of technical efficiency; even now it often seems to live in the shadow of the problem of productivity measurement (Schmidt 1985–1986).

Farrell's Contribution

The standard definition of technical inefficiency, first provided by M. J. Farrell (1957), can be explained in terms of figure 2.1. Assume that an activity is carried out under conditions of constant returns to scale. Then the unit isoquant shown in figure 2.1 describes the activity's technology in full as the minimum combinations of inputs (capital and labor) per unit of output required to produce one unit of the activity's output. If the relative prices of capital and labor are given by the line BC, then point A on YY indicates the least costly combination of inputs for producing any given quantity of the output. If the input combination used by a particular producer is represented by some

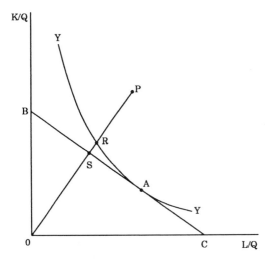

Figure 2.1.

other point, such as *P*, its inefficiency can be measured along the ray *OP* as the proportional excess cost of producing that output over the minimum attainable. Because any point on *BC* represents the same unit cost of production as at *A*, that excess is *PS/OS*. Farrell proposed that the excess could be partitioned into two components. *PR/OR* is the proportional excess cost of inputs used over the feasible minimum cost *(R)* of producing the given output using the input proportions indicated by *OP*. This is called "technical inefficiency." Although *R* is a technically efficient combination of inputs, it is not the least-cost combination if factor prices are *BC*. *RS/OS* indicates the proportional excess cost due to the use of inappropriate input proportions (too much capital and too little labor, as the figure is drawn). Farrell referred to this distortion of input proportions as "price inefficiency."[1] He showed that these concepts can be generalized to more than two inputs and suggested a method whereby the unit isoquant *YY* could be approximated from data on actual production units, when the technical information that it contains is not actually known.

Farrell's analysis leads naturally to the identification of a third type of inefficiency when his assumption of constant returns to scale is dropped. If returns to scale are not constant, production can take place at a point having the properties of *A* in figure 2.1 yet still be inefficient because at a different scale the activity could be carried on at lower input costs per unit of output. "Scale inefficiency" refers to

production carried on at scales either too small or too large to minimize costs of production.[2]

Some time elapsed before other researchers began to develop
Farrell's analysis and to apply methods of measuring technical inefficiency. Several families of methods ultimately emerged, opening
a number of options to the empirical researcher. They differ in
whether they assign a specific form to the production function and
whether they allow for the possibility that the best-practice production technique still yields an uncertain or random output.[3] Farrell's
methodology can be applied directly; one simply assumes constant
returns to scale and then uses data on inputs per unit of output to
trace a frontier unit isoquant analogous to YY in figure 2.1. The isoquant must be convex to the origin but otherwise needs to take no
particular shape. Such direct applications of Farrell's technique hold
interest mainly for their empirical results.

Applications: Deterministic Frontier Production Functions

Farrell also suggested estimating a frontier production function with a
specific parametric form, such as the Cobb-Douglas. This suggestion
was picked up by Aigner and Chu (1968), who specified a Cobb-
Douglas production frontier (which avoids imposing the assumption
of constant returns to scale) and required all observations to lie on or
below it. Programming techniques can then be used to estimate the
frontier production function from data on actual plants. The choice of
assumption about the form of the production function has a strong
influence on the conclusions reached about the degree of technical
inefficiency. This is clear from the consideration that the number of
observed units that appear to be fully efficient technically is generally
only as large as the number of parameters of the production function
to be estimated. Researchers have found only limited scope for re-
laxing the assumed form of the production function. Førsund and
Jansen (1977), for example, worked with a cost function that is homothetic but not constant returns. Førsund and Hjalmarsson (1979a,
1979b) relaxed the homogeneity assumption of the Cobb-Douglas
form to allow for biased technical change.

A difficulty with these parametric production frontiers is that no
test can be made of how well the production function fits the data
because the estimates resulting from the mathematical programming
techniques do not have known statistical properties. It was a natural

step to propose that observations of individual units' efficiency levels
be regarded as data points lying below a deterministic frontier drawn
from a one-sided statistical distribution. With the data assumed to
follow some particular one-sided distribution, statistical techniques
could be used to estimate the parameters of the frontier function.
Richmond (1974), following suggestions by Afriat (1972), proposed
the assumption that the residuals from a logarithmic production function follow the gamma distribution. Estimation of the production
frontier on this assumption provided a measure of the average
technical inefficiency of the observations. It was established that
maximum-likelihood estimators could be developed that correspond
to the programming techniques of Aigner and Chu (1968), yielding a
satisfactory statistical basis for estimating deterministic frontier production functions (Schmidt 1976; Greene 1980). Nonetheless, the
apparatus remained quite restrictive as a basis for inferring the extent
of inefficiency. The requirement of one-sided residuals still caused
the position of the estimated function to depend on a small number of
observations that might be inaccurately measured or otherwise
abnormal. And the form of the one-sided distribution imposed on the
data remained an arbitrary choice. A particular distribution such as
the gamma might prove to have attractive statistical properties
(Greene 1980), but no theory emerged to connect that distribution to
any specific economic process accounting for the pattern of observed
technical inefficiency.

Stochastic Frontier Production Function

The major development in this research that brings us to the methods
used in this study is the concept of a stochastic production frontier.
Although the long tradition of economic modeling of production has
stuck to a deterministic optimal relationship between inputs and the
output that emerges from them, there are compelling empirical
reasons for supposing that production processes that are optimally
planned ex ante still yield an output that is a random variable. The
weather is better or worse than the manager's mean expectation.
Equipment failures or product defects occur more or less frequently
than experience would predict. Inputs with variable qualities diverge
from mean expectations, or suppliers' random deliveries depart
abnormally from expected arrival times. In short, the input-output
relationship depends on a number of random variables for which

only the frequency distributions are likely to be known when production is planned—not the particular values that will emerge after production plans have been committed. These considerations support the assumption that the production frontier is itself stochastic and that particular outcomes may indeed lie above the frontier, when a producer has not only planned optimally but also enjoyed better-than-average drawings of the random variables. This plausible assumption leads to the "composed error" model of technical inefficiency, in which the stochastic production frontier may be written as:

$y = f(x)exp(v - u)$.

Here y represents output, $f(x)$ is the deterministic core of the frontier production function, v, is some symmetrical random error, and the one-sided error term $u \geq 0$ captures technical inefficiency.

This formulation, introduced by Aigner, Lovell, and Schmidt (1977) and Meeusen and van den Broeck (1977a), offers a number of compelling advantages. It allows room for errors of observation (preferably of the dependent variable, output). It avoids the earlier techniques' high sensitivity to errors in the data, which allows the nonstochastic production frontier to be grossly distorted by a single observation for which output is overestimated or input underestimated.[4] The stochastic production frontier permits the measurement errors to be subsumed in the symmetrical error component. Another advantage of the stochastic production frontier is to allow estimation by a simple procedure of corrected ordinary least squares. Once assumptions are made about the distributions of the composed-error components v and u, the production function can be estimated by ordinary least squares and then "corrected" for the downward pull of the mean technical inefficiency residual by an upward shift of the intercept. That is, the estimated production function after the correction is relocated so as to minimize the sum of squared residuals v.[5]

Of course, the problem remains of what distribution to assign to the residuals components v and u. As usual, the central limit theorem can be invoked to warrant assuming a normal distribution for v. No such consideration stands out to support any particular assumption about the one-sided residuals u, and statistical convenience and general plausibility continue to rule the roost.[6] Both half-normal (our choice) and exponential distributions have been employed. Fortunately the limited evidence available suggests that these two assumptions give rise to quite similar parameters for the estimated production frontier (Aigner, Lovell, and Schmidt 1977),[7] and one study indicates that the extent of technical inefficiency based on the two assumptions is highly correlated across industries (Corbo and de Melo 1983).

Various extensions of the stochastic production frontier methodology have emerged. Recall Farrell's distinction between technical inefficiency and price inefficiency. When a single equation for the production function is estimated, the assumption is implicitly made that each observed firm buys whatever inputs it deems appropriate in the light of their various prices in order to maximize profits. Indeed without some variation in the input mixes due to differences in input prices or other sources, the coefficients of the production function cannot be estimated with precision. But because firms can become inefficient by purchasing the wrong quantities of inputs (price inefficiency), even if the inputs are used optimally once bought (technical efficiency), it is desirable to test for price inefficiency and technical inefficiency at the same time. This can be done if the chosen form of the production function allows the derivation of input demand frontiers. Then if the researcher has data available on both the prices and quantities of inputs purchased by the observed firms, a system of equations representing the production (or cost) frontier and the factor-demand functions can be estimated and the incidence of both technical and price inefficiency determined from them (see Schmidt and Lovell 1979). Technical and price efficiency must still be assumed independent of each other—undesirably, because many sources of technical inefficiency (such as managerial competence) would surely be likely to affect the optimality of input-purchasing decisions as well.[8] One reason for the recent interest in using panel data to estimate frontier production functions lies in the possibility of avoiding this assumption (Schmidt 1985–1986). Because we lack data on key input prices even for the single year's data that we could utilize, we were confined to a single-equation approach to the measurement of technical efficiency alone.

Another line of innovation in the methodology has been to obtain inferences about whether an individual unit in the industry's population is efficient. Jondrow et al. (1982) provided a confidence interval for the unobserved one-sided error u_i conditional on the observed value of $(v_i - u_i)$, permitting statements about the probability that a given observation is technically inefficient (also see Waldman 1984).

2.2 Applications of Frontier Production Functions

Most econometric research on frontier production functions has been methodological in its orientation, and even many of the empirical papers have sought to display the methodology at work rather than to address any specific empirically founded question. Usable data were received with thanks from wherever they might come. Nonetheless, a number of empirical studies have been carried out—enough to impel that this review be selective (cf. Schmidt 1985–1986). Besides illustrating the present state of empirical applications, we explore the previous applications for conclusions helpful in framing our own investigation.

The origins of the data used in these empirical studies are strikingly far-flung. The methodology requires data on inputs and outputs of individual business units (enterprises or establishments). The disinclination of firms to hand these out to passers-by is well known, and in industrial countries the information is accessed by census agencies only under strict requirements of confidentiality. Accordingly many applications have been made to regulated industries in the industrial countries, for which the regulatory process exposes data on individual units, or to farms or large-numbers manufacturing industries, most located in developing countries, for which special data tabulations have been obtained by government agencies. While selected manufacturing industries have been studied in Sweden, Norway, Finland, the United Kingdom, France, and West Germany, the origins of most analyses are far-flung: regulated industries such as electric power and air and urban bus transportation in the United States; farms in the United States, India, the Philippines, and Tanzania; and selected manufacturing industries in Brazil, Chile, Colombia, Indonesia, and Taiwan. To say the least, generalization is a problem. Nonetheless, some findings merit summary.

How Much Technical Inefficiency Exists?

A natural question is the actual amount of technical efficiency found to exist. Empirical researchers have differed in their choices of research methods—not just the basic options for measuring technical efficiency but also the many options associated with the definition of variables, form of the production function, and even the method of stating the resulting inefficiency. Whether the differences among studies reflect true conditions in the sectors studied or different choices of methodology often cannot be determined. Nonetheless, a few findings are worth noting.

The first group holds interest because it responds to predictions from the basic methodology. We noted that deterministic frontier production functions are estimated on the assumption that all data points lie below the production frontier, while the stochastic function allows some units to appear more efficient than the estimated frontier. Deterministic frontiers should therefore deliver higher estimates of inefficiency than stochastic ones. This result was observed in at least one study that applied both methods to the same data set, U.S. electric power plants (Cowing, Reifschneider, and Stevenson 1983). Corbo and de Melo (1983) estimated mean levels of efficiency in forty-three Chilean manufacturing industries of only 43 percent relative to deterministic frontier but 72 to 81 percent when a stochastic frontier was employed. For ten French industries, Meeusen and van den Broeck (1977a) found a similar contrast between ranges of 47 and 72 percent and 71 and 94 percent. The levels of efficiency observed in studies using different data sets are consistent with this pattern (Schmidt 1985–1986, pp. 318–319). In the same way, employing more flexible production functions (translog, versus Cobb-Douglas) has led to higher estimates of efficiency (Kopp and Smith 1980), expected because the flexible form envelops the data more closely (Schmidt 1985–1986, p. 319).

What are the efficiency levels actually estimated? We can report on one group of estimates that use the stochastic function, the same method of expressing technical efficiency, and appear not to differ importantly in other research methods. Lee and Tyler (1978) estimated 62.5 percent efficiency for Brazilian manufacturing industries, Tyler and Lee (1979) about 55 percent for Colombian apparel and footwear industries, Pitt and Lee (1981) 62 to 68 percent for Indonesia's weaving industry, and Meeusen and van den Broeck (1977a) 71 to 94 percent for ten French manufacturing industries. Are these estimates close or scattered? No one can say, but they at least suggest that—if one buys the methodology—enough inefficiency exists to make the matter well worth studying.

Does Efficiency Differ Predictably among Units?

A number of studies have tested hypotheses about the efficiency levels of different types of units within their populations. Are large firms more efficient than small ones? Are businesses controlled by multinational enterprises more efficient than domestic firms. Are export-oriented firms more efficient than those producing import substitutes? Are state-owned enterprises less efficient than privately owned ones? We summarize the answers selectively in order to give a feeling for the questions that have been asked. There is too little consensus and replication to reach strong conclusions about efficiency differences among units.

Seitz (1971), analyzing the efficiency of electric generating stations in their first year of operation, concluded that technical efficiency depends mainly on vintage effects—the ability of plants constructed later to utilize more advanced technology. Similarly Jondrow et al. (1982) concluded that the (probabilistically) efficient plants are large and of recent vintage but do not employ large quantities of capital relative to fuel or labor. Studies of manufacturing industries in developing countries reached the same conclusion (Pitt and Lee 1981; Chen and Tang 1987). Caves, Christensen, and Tretheway (1981) associated the efficiency of U.S. airlines with high load factors and long stage lengths. Müller (1974) concluded that differences in farmers' stocks of information explain the varying efficiency levels in U.S. agriculture, and he found that information stocks do not affect the productivity of capital and other factors differentially. Shapiro and Müller (1977) associated technical efficiency in developing-country agriculture with overall modernization and with better information stocks (which increase the output elasticity of labor but not of land).

Other investigations have shed light on the relationship between the sizes of plants or firms and their technical efficiency. Todd (1971) calculated Farrell efficiency frontiers for (rather aggregated) British manufacturing industries, observing that small firms account for some of the points on each estimated frontier, invariably because they use efficient input combinations that are more labor intensive than those of large firms. Yotopoulos and Lau (1973) concluded that small farms in India are more efficient technically than are large ones, although the two groups show no difference in price efficiency. Meller (1976) provided the most elaborate investigation of scale and efficiency in manufacturing industries, disaggregating each of twenty-one Chilean industries into five size-classes of establishments. He estimated a separate efficiency frontier for each size class in each industry. Although the larger plants did not typically exhibit efficiency frontiers superior to those of their smaller competitors, he did conclude that the extent of technical inefficiency of small plants with respect to their own efficiency frontiers was much greater than for large plants.[9] Meeusen and van den Broeck (1977b) similarly observed higher efficiency levels in the larger French manufacturing companies. Chen and Tang (1987) used a production function that allows the degree of scale economies to be determined empirically. They found that larger firms were more efficient, but the difference was not significant statistically.

Schmidt (1985–1986, pp. 317–318) made the point that hypotheses about the differential efficiency levels of subspecies among an industry's members do not require the forntier production function methodology, only the standard tests for intercept or slope shifts employed in the estimation of a conventional production function. The interindustry approach taken in our own study makes more intrinsic use of the methodology because efficiency levels cannot otherwise be compared across industries with putatively different production functions.

Are Relative Efficiency Levels Sensitive to Measurement Errors?

Because our study seeks to explain efficiency differences among industries, an important question is the similarity of rankings obtained for sets of industries through different methods of measurement. The results of Corbo and de Melo (1983) show how closely correlated are estimates of technical efficiency calculated by different methods for a fixed sample of industries. The correlation between stochastic frontier production functions using the half-normal and exponential distributions is high, 0.854. However, the correlations between stochastic frontier estimates and those using various methods that constrain all residuals to be one-sided are much lower—0.589 down to −0.142. Thus, substantive conclusions about the extent of technical inefficiency and its behavioral determinants are likely to differ a good deal depending on whether the stochastic frontier methodology or some other is employed.

Are Units' Efficiency Levels Stable over Time?

Several studies have investigated the stability of inefficiency patterns over time. Førsund and Hjalmarsson (1979a) and Albach (1980) found that the identities of the most efficient firms stay relatively constant over time, which suggests that efficiency rests on stable factors and not transient components or elements of luck. Albach concluded that average inefficiency in the German chemical industry appears to be higher in boom periods when investment activity is high, suggesting shakedown problems with new equipment and/or the use of inefficient equipment or procedures that lead to rising marginal costs for some firms when peak demand is being served. Pitt and Lee (1981) tested three hypotheses about firms' efficiency levels over time: time invariance, independence, and an intermediate case allowing some persistence of effect. The last hypothesis was accepted.

A good deal of evidence associates the changes in units' relative efficiency ratings to capital vintage effects: once shaken down, a new production unit tends to have a top efficiency ranking, but over time it slides down the rankings as newer units embody more advanced technologies that cannot be economically retrofitted.[10] We shall test this hypothesis.

Do Estimated Functions Reveal Sources of Inefficiency?

Certain interesting conclusions result from comparing the coefficients of frontier production functions (estimated by linear-programming or maximum-likelihood techniques) to those of production functions fitted to the same data using ordinary regression techniques. The frontier function represents best practice, while the other roughly indicates technological relationships observed in average practice.[11] Differences between the coefficients of the functions are taken to indicate differences between best-practice units and others. In their analysis of the Norwegian woodpulp industry, Førsund and Jansen (1977) found that the capital-labor ratios of best-practice plants are markedly higher than those of other plants, consistent with best practice involving more capital and newer vintages of equipment. Albach (1980) obtained a similar result in German chemical firms, but Meller (1976) did not find a systematic pattern in Chilean manufacturing industries. Lee and Tyler (1978) developed a maximum-likelihood estimate of the frontier production function for Brazilian manufacturing firms, concluding that the output elasticity of capital is higher on the frontier than in average practice (also Tyler 1979). This result also suggests an association between efficiency and capital intensity because the output elasticity equals an input's share of total cost (in perfect competition with constant returns to scale). A similar pattern appears in the analysis of French manufacturing industries by Meeusen and van den Broeck (1977a), who found some indication that industries with higher efficiency levels exhibit higher output elasticities of capital. This appearance of the pattern when the comparison extends across industries (rather than across competing firms within an industry) suggests that efficiency may be easier to achieve in industries with capital-intensive technologies, whatever the effect of using assorted amounts and vintages of equipment in individual plants.

Why Does Technical Efficiency Differ among Industries?

We now come to the empirical question central to our own investigation: the reasons that estimated levels of technical efficiency may differ among industries. Only a few investigators have previously tested hypotheses about interindustry differences. Downie (1958), using a method with some resemblance to Farrell's technique, concluded that the less efficient British manufacturing industries displayed a conjunction of high seller concentration with collusive market agreements (such as price fixing). Carlsson (1972) investigated a number of determinants of technical inefficiency in Swedish manufacturing industries, concluding that inefficiency is positively related to tariff protection and negatively related to seller concentration (possibly because of the common underlying influence of scale economies, which are more important in the more efficient industries). He also found that industries producing more heterogeneous lines of products appear less efficient, a result expected when products are differentiated and some producers have happened upon more profitable varieties than have others.[12] Timmer (1971) found that the inefficiency indexes of the various states' agricultural sectors could be related to several factors, such as the extent of off-farm work done by farmers (see also Beeson and Husted 1989).

2.3 Methods Used in This Study: The Production Function

The methods outlined for measuring technical inefficiency are generally independent of the specific production function chosen for estimation. In this section we explore the form we selected and the process for estimating each industry's average technical inefficiency.

Options

Various theoretical production functions are available. We shall write three familiar ones in the forms normally employed for statistical estimation, which show the relationships among them with particular clarity. In general, we suppose that the net output of a production process Q depends on the quantities of services of factors of production that are employed: $Q = F(K, L)$ where K indicates the flow of capital services and L the flow of labor services. The familiar Cobb-Douglas production function then becomes $Q = AK^{\alpha}L^{\beta}$, or in the form that will be used in this study, $Q/L = A(K/L)^{\alpha}L^{\alpha + \beta - 1}$. Written in logarithms for convenient statistical estimation, the Cobb-Douglas production function becomes:

$$\ln(Q/L) = a_0 + a_1 \ln (K/L) + a_2 \ln L.$$

Another production function popular in recent years is the constant-elasticity-of-substitution (CES) form, written as follows (in the approximation popularized by Kmenta 1967):

$$\ln (Q/L) = b_0 + b_1 \ln (K/L) + b_2 \ln L + b_3(\ln (K/L))^2.$$

The third form that has received widespread use is the transcendental logarithmic (translog) form, written in a similar manner as:

$$\ln(Q/L) = c_0 + c_1 \ln (K/L) + c_2 \ln L + c_3(\ln (K/L))^2 + c_4(\ln L)^2 + c_5(\ln (K/L))(\ln L).$$

The translog function serves as a consistent second-order approximation to any production function that takes the form $\ln Q = F(\ln K, \ln L)$ (Denny and Fuss 1977). From the preceding expressions, it is obvious that the CES form generalizes the Cobb-Douglas, and the translog generalizes the CES. Put another way, statistically insignificant coefficients for c_4 and c_5 in the estimation of the translog function can tell us that the CES is a satisfactory representation of the production process in question, and the insignificance of b_3 in the estimated CES function brings us back to the Cobb-Douglas form.

Considerations Governing Choice

The production function employed in this study was chosen partly from exploratory evidence but ultimately on a priori grounds. The more flexible forms reduce the threat of mismeasuring technical inefficiency for industries whose production functions depart substantially from the simple Cobb-Douglas. On the other hand, the estimation of flexible forms consumes more degrees of freedom, potentially reducing the precision with which parameters of the production function can be estimated or even precluding estimation for some industries with very few establishments contributing data to the Bureau of the Census. The essential question is whether the gain from using a more flexible form offsets the cost in fewer degrees of freedom.

An argument can be made for taking the simplest approach and selecting the Cobb-Douglas. It has apparently fit the data well in many studies made on a wide variety of industrial processes. Griliches and Ringstad (1971) found little explanatory gain in going from the Cobb-Douglas to the CES function. Some economists raise theoretical objections to the translog function because it need not be well behaved for every possible combination of inputs; output need not increase monotonically with all inputs, and isoquants need not be everywhere convex (Berndt and Christensen 1973).[13] Nonetheless, previous empirical evidence and considerations of research design do make a case for the use of the translog form in this project.

The empirical consideration that inclines us toward the translog form is the copious evidence that manufacturing production functions commonly prove nonhomothetic in the use of capital. That is, for given prices of capital and labor, the optimal capital-labor ratio seems to increase with the scale of operation. Although this point has received little attention from econometricians specializing in the estimation of production functions (compare Todd 1971), the empirical evidence strongly confirms the pattern. Davis (1956), who cited a number of earlier studies, found strong evidence that capital intensity increases with scale in the majority of the industries he examined (see also Shen 1965). Caves and Pugel (1980) used data on companies' ratios of depreciable assets to sales (from Internal Revenue Service) to conclude that capital intensity increases with scale for about 90 percent of manufacturing industries.[14] Because most evidence on the point comes from company accounts rather than establishment records,[15] (backward) vertical integration may account for part of the pattern. Overall it seems unacceptable to employ a production function that imposes homotheticity.

This evidence is, of course, related to the research in the field of econometrics on the presence of separability—whether marginal rates of substitution between pairs of factors in a separated group are independent of the levels of factors outside the group. The tests reported in the literature are complex, and they often utilize data aggregated over a number of distinct industrial activities, making the results difficult to evaluate, On the one hand, some tests of reasonably disaggregated sectors fail to reject weak global separability (equivalent to a test of Cobb-Douglas technology) for the majority of industries (Corbo and Meller 1979); on the other hand, separability gains rather little support in tests run on U.S. manufacturing as a whole (Denny and Fuss 1977). It seems fair to conclude that separability conditions consistent with Cobb-Douglas technology are not accepted with sufficient frequency to warrant considering the translog production function a needless refinement.[16]

Another consideration favoring the translog form comes from the evidence on scale economies in manufacturing. All forms allow for the possibility of scale economies. However, Cobb-Douglas and CES constrain the scale economies to take the form of a constant elasticity, whereas the translog form allows their extent to vary with the scale of operation. Broadly based estimates of Cobb-Douglas and CES production functions in manufacturing (such as Griliches 1968; Griliches and Ringstad 1971) typically find statistically significant economies of scale. However, a considerable weight of evidence from the field of industrial organization suggests that plant cost curves in narrowly defined manufacturing industries typically take the shape of a letter *J* lying on its side—indicating scale economies (which may or may not be substantial) at small scales of operation that diminish and give way to constant returns over an extensive range of large scales (see Weiss 1976, for example). The quadratic terms in the translog form potentially allow this effect to be approximated, whereas the other forms imply that scale economies (if any) persist uniformly through the observed range of outputs. Again the translog form alone seems able to encompass an important empirical regularity.

A final merit of the translog function was noted above. Because of its flexibility, it reduces the risk of inferring technical inefficiency where the problem instead is a poor fit to the data of a more restrictive form.

The specific function used to approximate production frontiers in this study will therefore be a version of the translog form, differing from that listed above only in that materials inputs are included as a principal category of input, and output is measured as the sale value of gross output. The form is:

$$\ln(GO/L) = a_0 + a_1 \ln(K/L) + a_2 \ln(M/L) + a_3 \ln N + a_4(\ln K/L)^2$$
$$+ a_5(\ln M/L)^2 + a_6(\ln N)^2 + a_7 (\ln K/L)(\ln M/L)$$
$$+ a_8(\ln K/L)(\ln N) + a_9(\ln M/L)(\ln N) + a_i X_i + u.$$

Here GO is shipments plus increase in finished good inventories, M is purchased inputs, N is total employees, L is a measure of labor hours, and K is book value of capital. X_i are other additive variables, included to test the assumed homogeneity of the principal input categories just listed (a procedure employed by Griliches and Ringstad 1971). They are explained in chapter 3 along with the definitions of the input categories. For now, we can say that the variables conform to the data available on manufacturing establishments covered by the Annual Survey of Manufactures.

The appropriateness of including materials inputs as one of the basic categories is treated as an open question. However, on the basis of evidence reviewed in chapter 4, we ultimately rely chiefly on the corresponding production function form with $ln\ (VA/L)$ as the dependent variable. Many econometric studies of production functions exclude materials, a procedure appropriate if either there is no substitution between purchased inputs and the primary factors of production (capital and labor) or there is perfect substitution between materials inputs and primary factors. Neither assumption is attractive a priori, and we were specifically concerned that technical inefficiency may be related to certain aspects of their use. For example, industries making heavy use of energy inputs have experienced important changes in relative input prices since 1973, and the production technologies of their individual establishments may have adapted to this change in varying degrees.

The preferred method for estimating translog production functions is in the form of a system of relationships that embody the side conditions for profit maximization in competitive product and factor markets. The system includes a basic production or cost function and a semilogarithmic equation for each input relating its cost share to its price (for example, Christensen and Greene 1976). The information available on the broad population of U.S. manufacturing industries does not include factor prices except for production-worker labor and so does not permit the estimation of the cost-share equations. Accordingly we cannot employ the research methods that would allow the investigation of technical inefficiency and price inefficiency together (Schmidt and Lovell 1979).[17] Furthermore, when a single equation is estimated for the production function, bias may result because the business units in fact choose their inputs and plan their outputs simultaneously, so that it is inappropriate to assume that outputs depend on exogenously chosen inputs. The simultaneity problem is thus injected, and estimation of the production frontier by means of ordinary least squares leads to biased and inconsistent estimates of the coefficients.

Unfortunately there is no practicable way around this problem, and we simply utilize ordinary least squares (OLS) and invoke for the formulation suggested by Zellner, Kmenta, and Dreze (1966) to rationalize the procedure: the production function is made stochastic with a disturbance representing purely random elements, on the assumption that the entrepreneur cannot know the effect of the disturbance until after the quantities of inputs have been preselected.[18] The procedure further assumes that the prices of output and inputs either are known with certainty or are statistically independent of the production-function disturbance and that entrepreneurs maximize the mathematical expectation of profit.

The procedure chosen for estimating the technical inefficiency of each manufacturing industry thus involves a correction to the OLS estimate of the production function, adjusting the intercept of the estimated function for the estimated mean of the asymmetrical component of the composed residuals (corrected OLS, or COLS). This is the particular version of the composed-error approach to stochastic production frontiers proposed by Aigner, Schmidt, and Lovell (1977). With the Zellner-Kmenta-Dreze assumption in place, it can be shown that the existence of the composed error term biases only the constant term in the OLS regression.

3

Estimation of Frontier Production Functions: Exploratory Analyses

Applying the methodology of frontier production functions to a large number of manufacturing industries is a daunting task. On the one hand, although many applications have been made to individual sets of data on producer groups, there is no body of codified experience with the results of the technique. The literature review in chapter 2 offers little guidance concerning the likely consequences of various tactical choices. On the other hand, many tactical choices must be made as to the form of the production function, method of estimation, and definitions of the various variables. In the absence of a budget constraint, one would estimate stochastic frontier production functions in as many alternative forms as are needed to determine how sensitive the outcomes are to the various tactical choices. That luxury was unavailable; the budget constraint permitted only a limited range of alternative computations. In this chapter we describe the preliminary steps that were undertaken to determine the best procedures to follow.

3.1 Initial Choices

Certain parameters were set at the beginning by the basic design of the project. It was confined to manufacturing industries in the United States. The latter restriction sounds innocuous, but it is in fact not. The methodology requires that the collection of units comprising the "industry" embrace at least some that are efficient enough meaningfully to identify the efficient frontier. This assumption does not seem outrageous, given the U.S. international standing in productivity and real-income levels, despite the recent furor over the nation's international competitiveness. Nonetheless, it is a substantial, if practically unavoidable, assumption.[1]

Manufacturing industries were chosen because their input-output relationships match well to our theoretical concept of a production function, because they tend to serve national or international markets, and because their large number is congenial to our approach of cross-section inference. The four-digit level of the Standard Industrial Classification was chosen on the view, based on considerable research in industrial economics, that this level of aggregation matches an economic definition of the market better than any other. At the same time, we decided not to expend effort evaluating the appropriateness of definitions of the individual four-digit industries. Their heterogeneities in product mix, geographic submarkets, and the like are potentially important for the analysis of technical efficiency, but we preferred to control for such differences in the second stage of the analysis by means of variables that measure these sources of heterogeneity. The full set of approximately 450 industries was taken as the potential sample for analysis, subject to exclusions described below.[2]

Establishments, not firms, would be the units of observation.[3] This choice could be justified on the grounds of data availability alone; however, we were equally concerned with the high level of diversification (at the four-digit level of disaggregation) that marks large U.S. industrial enterprises. The methodology of the frontier production function makes no sense unless the observed entities are quite specialized to the activity in question. Even plants pose a problem of diversification beyond a single four-digit industry, but a much smaller one, and we have controls for that source of noise. Many of the economic hypotheses about technical efficiency apply jointly to firms and to the plants they operate. Others are specific to the production apparatus and thus address themselves to plants. Finally, we can control in the cross-section phase of the study for interindustry differences in the relation between plants and firms, for example, the extent of multiplant operation and enterprise-level diversification.

A single year's data would be employed for the analysis, it was decided, and 1977 was selected.[4] No year in the 1970s has much claim to being called normal, but 1977 offered better qualifications than most others. More important, it was a year when the Census of Manufactures was taken. Although the necessary data were available for other years, 1977 possessed the advantage that variables published in the Census of Manufactures would serve as coterminous exogenous variables in the analysis of interindustry differences in technical efficiency.

Although 1977 was a Census of Manufacturers year, the full set of establishments classified to each industry by the Census was not used to estimate the production function. Rather, in order to secure certain necessary variables, the establishments utilized were only those included in the Annual Survey of Manufacturers (ASM) panel, which report data on several variables (notably capital stocks) collected only from establishments included in the ASM panel. The ASM panel includes all establishments employing 250 or more, plus a sample of smaller plants (the sampling frequency increasing with size).

Most variables measuring inputs and outputs were defined in ways that correspond directly to the data collected by the Bureau of the Census. Output for the establishment was defined as value of shipments plus the increase in finished-goods inventories between the beginning and end of the year. Capital was defined as the average of stocks of machinery, structures, and inventories at the beginning and end of the year; to this average was added an estimate of the capitalized values of leased buildings and equipment, on the assumption of a forty-year life for structures, a thirteen-year life for equipment, and a 12 percent rate of discount. Numbers of employees were taken as averages over the year (the problems of aggregating production and nonproduction employees and allowing for variations in hours worked are discussed below).

While we kept open the particular form of the production function (subject to the considerations discussed in section 2.3), we did decide at the outset to utilize only ordinary-least-squares estimation and to attempt the measurement only of technical, not price (allocative), efficiency. These choices were mandated by the budget constraint and accessible computing capabilities, as well as by the lack of input-price data. Also passed up were other potentially interesting refinements of the methodology, such as allowing the distribution of technical inefficiency to be truncated other than at its midpoint (and thereby avoiding the assumption that the modal level of technical inefficiency is zero) (Stevenson 1980).

3.2 Production Function Form and Definitions of Variables

Exploratory Procedure

Because of resource constraints on the number of tactical alternatives for estimating frontier production functions, we selected a panel of industries for experimentation, determining the final specifications for analyzing the full sample from what had been revealed by analysis of the panel. To minimize the obvious risk inherent in this procedure, we chose a dozen industries that seemed representative in several senses. They included both consumer and producer goods, durables and nondurables, industries serving local markets and others serving national markets. They contained widely varying numbers of plants reporting to the Bureau of the Census. The panel was consciously unrepresentative only in leaning toward large industries. It comprised these industries:

2011   Meat-packing plants

2026   Fluid milk

2052   Cookies and crackers

2086   Bottled and canned soft drinks

2281   Yarn-spinning mills

2541   Wood partitions, shelving, locker, and office and store furniture

3211   Flat glass

3273   Ready-mix concrete

3312   Blast furnaces, steelworks, and rolling mills

3465   Automotive stampings

3541   Machine tools, metal-cutting types

For each of these industries we estimated stochastic frontier production functions varying in the following ways:

1. Transcendental logarithmic (translog) or Cobb-Douglas functional form.

2. Gross output or value added (each divided by labor input) as the dependent variable; correspondingly, with materials inputs included or excluded.

3. Labor input measured as total employees or as equivalent production worker hours, using relative compensation of production and nonproduction workers to convert the latter's services into commensurable units.

We examined various properties of the resulting estimates, including the goodness of fit of each variant, the sensitivity of the inefficiency estimates obtained, and whether the skewness of the residuals indicated that technical inefficiency could be estimated. This last property is important and requires a brief explanation. Technical inefficiency is inferred from the skewness of the residuals around the fitted production function; the model in essence assumes that conventional random error is normally (symmetrically) distributed, while the technical-inefficiency component accounts for the skewness. Under two sets of circumstances, technical inefficiency cannot be measured from the observed residuals, the empirically important case being the one in which the residuals are skewed in the wrong direction. Even if one believes that some technical inefficiency exists in most industries, wrong-signed skewness is not implausible, if only because the normality of the random residuals is assumed to hold for the population but not necessarily for the sample. However, a substantial proportion of such cases in a sample of industries would certainly call the basic methodology into question.[5] Therefore the proportion of industries for which technical inefficiency could be estimated was treated as an important property of the various alternative procedures.

The results indicated clear choices in some cases, close calls in others. The translog form gave higher coefficients of determination (corrected for degrees of freedom) and made the calculation of technical inefficiency feasible somewhat more often than did the Cobb-Douglas form. This confirmed our a priori preference for the translog. Equations with gross output as the dependent variable fared much less well than those with value added, generating unstable estimates of technical inefficiency.[6] The choice between measuring labor by employees and by equivalent production-worker hours could not be resolved on the statistical evidence, although we did observe that the former indicates the presence of more technical inefficiency with three-to-one frequency.

We also examined standardized residuals for each industry and regression model. The minimum and maximum values of these proved quite revealing. They displayed a wider range for the models with gross output as the dependent variable, supporting other evidence adverse to that option. More important for the subsequent interpretation of our results, we observed a close association between the range of the residuals and whether technical inefficiency could be measured. As we noted, the common pattern precluding the estimation of technical inefficiency is an inappropriate skewness of the residuals from the fitted production function. Using the extreme values of the standardized residuals, we calculated the difference between the maximum positive residual for each model and the absolute value of the extreme negative residual. A positive difference, or a positive value above some threshold (depending on the model), was closely associated with the impossibility of estimating technical inefficiency (due to an implied negative variance for the asymmetrical distribution). This sensitivity of technical inefficiency to extreme values of the residuals is cautionary in general with regard to the methodology and assumes importance on a particular point of interpretation at a later stage.

Another diagnostic procedure employed in these exploratory runs was to include as linear regressors variables describing the composition of various categories of inputs or other aspects of the heterogeneity of the establishments classified to an industry. Significant coefficients for these variables indicate errors of aggregation in the inputs or other factors that could affect the estimated coefficients of the production function and thus the apparent extent of technical inefficiency (Griliches and Ringstad 1971). These control variables were:

1. Machinery divided by total capital.

2. Nonproduction workers divided by total employment.

3. Goods purchased for resale divided by total materials costs.

4. Cost of energy (fuels and electricity) divided by total materials costs.

5. Inventories divided by total capital.

6. Production-worker hours divided by total production workers (an indicator of the extent of part-time working).

7. Shipments of the establishment's most important seven-digit product divided by shipments classified to the four-digit industry containing that product (inverse measure of diversification).

In most cases it is obvious why these terms might reveal some inappropriate aggregation. The input categories that they distinguish are clearly not perfect substitutes for each other in most activities, and/or their use in the plant cannot be quickly adjusted to changing conditions.

On the basis of the counts of significant coefficients for these variables in the twelve-industry panel, we elected to retain the machinery proportion of total capital and the fuels proportion of materials inputs in the model for the analysis of the full sample of industries. These two variables and also inventories divided by total capital were significant in about one-third of the exploratory runs, while the remaining variables were almost never significant. We decided against including both machinery and inventories as proportions of total assets because of the built-in collinearity between them.

Choices of Research Procedure

Let us now consolidate the decisions reached from our explorations of the twelve-industry panel. Two versions would be estimated of the stochastic frontier production function for each industry that contains an adequate number of plant observations. One would employ gross output in the dependent variable, and it would involve labor input measured by total employees. The other would employ value added as the dependent variable, and labor input would be measured as equivalent production-worker hours. Despite the inferior performance in the panel of production functions with gross output as the dependent variable (and materials included among the inputs), the potential importance of efficiency in the use of materials at the plant level seemed great enough to warrant retaining gross output in the analysis. The two labor-input measures were lined up to include the conceptually superior one with value added, the simpler one with gross output (where the problem of simultaneous determination of input and output, already severe, would not be amplified by the joint determination of output and hours worked). The machinery component of total capital and the fuels component of purchased materials were included as additive regressors in both models.

Four-digit SIC industries differ widely in their total numbers of plants and thus how many are covered in the Annual Survey of Manufactures. We decided, given the numbers of regressors in the models to be estimated for the full sample of industries, to exclude those with fewer than twenty plants meeting all qualifications for incorporation. Most industries contain far more than this minimum number, and that suggested two extensions of the analysis dealing with different-sized plants. First, a good deal of empirical evidence shows that the variance of profits of small companies exceeds that of large ones (e.g., Sherman 1968), and so we suspected that small plants within industries might show greater technical inefficiency. Second, we considered the possibility of inferring the extent of scale economies from the fitted production functions so that we could evaluate efficiency in the attainment of cost-minimizing scales of production alongside the analysis of technical inefficiency.

The idea of an intensive examination of scale economies was dropped after the results for the twelve-industry panel were analyzed. The behavior of the estimated coefficients, especially in the translog functions, did not inspire confidence in our ability to determine the minimum efficient scales of the bulk of four-digit manufacturing industries using such a blanket approach. Differentiating between technical efficiency in large and small plants, however, continued to seem a promising line of investigation. In the exploratory study we divided those industries with more than sixty plants into their larger and smaller halves (on the basis of total employment) and estimated the frontier production functions separately for each.

3.3 Quality of Data

A sensitive question for the estimation of frontier production functions and technical inefficiency is the quality of the underlying data on individual manufacturing establishments. One reason for preferring stochastic frontier production functions to other methods for inferring efficiency frontiers is that the stochastic frontier makes allowance for random errors in the measurement of output. But it is immune to such errors only if they are in fact random, and measurement errors in input variables are a source of trouble in any case.

Sensitivity of Data-Editing Procedures

The reason that the technical-inefficiency measure is sensitive to data errors is apparent from the structure of the model. Technical inefficiency is inferred from asymmetry in the residuals around a conventional fitted production function, and its calculation rests on the higher moments of these residuals. A large positive data error in the measurement of a single plant's output becomes magnified in the process and can either increase the extent of estimated technical inefficiency (by raising its industry's estimated frontier) or make inefficiency appear nonexistent (by reversing the skewness of the residuals). A large understatement of an important input will have the same effect. Therefore it is imperative to correct or remove observations that seem with a high probability to involve data errors. On the other hand, the loss involved from removing a correct but outlying observation on the presumption of a data error is very large. It is important that plants that are actually very efficient carry their weight in determining the estimated efficiency frontier. It is equally important that estimated average inefficiency reflect the performance of any plants that are extremely inefficient. These considerations make the investigator's choice of data-editing rules a sensitive one, especially because the frontier production functions could not be reestimated under a series of alternative data-editing rules.

Related to this problem is the question whether to exclude establishments that supply accurate data but exhibit abnormalities that make them inappropriate subjects for the analysis of technical efficiency. A good example is a plant that began or ceased operation in the year under study. The shakedown process for a new plant involves an economic inefficiency that (up to a point) is unavoidable. There is a case for excluding start-up plants if their teething troubles are viewed as essentially a fact of life. The case for excluding them is strengthened by the measurement problems that they raise: their stocks of capital are used for only a fraction of the year, but the fraction is unknown. Symmetrical problems arise for plants closed in the course of the year. And many other problems of this type arise. A number of editing rules were applied to exclude plants that are inappropriate for the sample even if their activities were measured correctly.

The following sections report on the additional data-editing rules devised for this project and their consequences for the establishments available for analysis. These rules were chosen on the basis of both a priori considerations and analysis of descriptive statistics on the twelve industries used to pretest aspects of the procedure for calculating stochastic frontier production functions.

Zero Values of Key Variables

One obvious basis for excluding establishments from the analysis was the reporting of zero values for gross output or principal inputs. Plants reporting zero values of gross output, labor input or capital were omitted. No manufacturing plant can be presumed in steady-state operation without reporting positive values of these variables (quite apart from the fact that their logarithms are undefined). Technical inefficiency is most reasonably assessed for ongoing plants that are economically viable for appreciable periods of time. In this same spirit plants reporting zero or negative value added were also excluded.

In order to exclude plants that make no use of key inputs, those that report no machinery in their capital stock components or no production workers were deleted. Such plants could otherwise remain in the sample if they reported, respectively, positive total capital (due to buildings, inventories) or positive labor input (due to nonproduction workers). A plant using no machinery or no production workers was deemed to be either subject to an error in data or atypical of the manufacturing activity to which it is classified.

Plants Unsuited to Research Design

We excluded any plant that reported a zero capital stock at the beginning or the end of the year. This rule is intended to eliminate plants beginning operation or being closed and dismantled during the year. They are omitted in order to confine the assessment of technical inefficiency to plants viable over a significant period of time. Plants employing fewer than four workers were also excluded on the conjecture that such small operations are unlikely to be carrying on activities comparable to the larger establishments classified to their industries. Also any errors in the data reported by such plants might well be large proportionally. Furthermore their data are more likely to be estimated by the Census Bureau rather than obtained by survey.[7]

Presumptive Data Errors

Various restrictions were imposed in the form of consistency checks that indicate where some datum submitted by a plant does not lie within a credible range and is therefore presumed in error. The following classes of observations were dropped:

1. Reported capital expenditures for the year were more than twice the average of beginning- and end-of-year capital stocks. Such a plant has either reported its capital expenditures or capital stock incorrectly or made a major acquisition and divestment of plant and equipment in a short period of time. Even if the reported data should be correct, as in the latter case, such a plant may be deemed too far out of equilibrium to contribute usefully to the analysis.

2. Reported average wage payments per production worker for the year were less than $1. Given levels of market money wages and the statutory minimum wage prevailing in 1977, an average hourly wage below $1 indicates either a data error or some quite unusual compensation arrangements. The plant's reported input of production worker labor is not necessarily in error in such cases, but such a plant should still be excluded. Although employee compensation does not enter directly into the calculation of frontier production functions, it does enter indirectly in the process of converting inputs of nonproduction labor into production worker equivalents (by means of relative annual compensation).

3. Plants were dropped if they reported average annual hours per production worker in excess of 4,500, which corresponds to 90 hours a week (with a 50-week working year). Even if the number of production workers is reported correctly by such a plant, the putative error in hours worked distorts the analysis indirectly in the calculation of production-worker-equivalent hours worked by all employees.

4. Plants that report average annual compensation of nonproduction workers of less than $1,000 or more than $100,000 were excluded. These limits were selected judgmentally to lie outside the range of reasonably plausible steady-state values. Once again, the (putative) error could lie either in the reported number of nonproduction workers or in their compensation. The former error would distort estimated total employment at the plant, the latter the calculation of production-worker-equivalent hours.

5. Even after the data exclusions already listed, large variances in the calculated variables that enter into the stochastic frontier production functions were found to imply enormous differences in some pilot industries between plants' reported maximum and minimum values. These are the ratios of gross output, value added, and capital stock to the number of persons employed or to production-worker-equivalent hours. It seems implausible that such raw measures of labor productivity or input structure could differ among comparable and competing plants by a hundredfold. Unlike the previous exclusion rules, in this case the suspect magnitudes cannot be checked against reference standards drawn from general knowledge. Therefore any exclusion rule must rest on the suspected data point's position in the distribution of that variable for other plants classified to the industry.

Table 3.1
Indicators of relative importance of various rules for excluding establishments from estimation of frontier production functions

Number	Number of industries with no rejections	Number of industries rule resulting in maximum rejections
1. Fewer than four employees	6	21
2. No production workers	15	2
3. No production worker hours	19	1
4. No production worker payroll	17	2
5. No shipments	20	1
6. No purchased materials	17	1
7. No capital	46	0
8. No gross output	40	0
9. Labor input less than four man-years	7	19
10. No materials used	28	0
11. Gross output per employee more than 4.5 standard deviations over sample mean	11	6
12. Total capital per employee more than 4.5 standard deviations over sample mean	8	2
13. Total materials per employee more than 4.5 standard deviations over sample mean	7	19
14. No machinery	21	4
15. No production workers	15	2
16. Hours per production worker over 4,500 annually	302	1

17. Annual compensation per nonproduction worker less than $1,000 or over $100,000	4	257
18. Production worker average was under $1 an hour	14	6
19. Capital expenditure more than twice average beginning, ending capital stocks	363	0
20. No machinery either beginning or end of year	4	68
21. No inventories beginning of year	11	36
22. No inventories end of year	63	1
23. Negative value added	15	20

Heeding the sensitivity of our research method to large positive errors in these variables, we employed the following reasoning. A wide variety of evidence indicates that, as a descriptive matter, the absolute sizes of plants and firms in an industry (whether measured by output or principal inputs) tend to be well represented by the lognormal distribution. Because ratios of lognormally distributed variables are also distributed lognormally, as an approximation, the logarithms of these variables for plants in a given four-digit industry can be assumed to be normally distributed. The problem is therefore to truncate the upper tail of the distribution of these variables, when measured in natural units, at a reasonable number of standard deviations in the corresponding (presumed) normal distribution of the logarithms. The means and standard deviations of the labor-productivity variables actually observed in the twelve-industry panel were used to estimate the approximate mean and standard deviation of the corresponding lognormal distribution. From these we could estimate approximately where the upper tail of the lognormal distribution of the variable would be truncated by cutting off observations exceeding any given number of measured standard deviations above the mean. The rule selected excludes observations that exceed 4.5 calculated standard deviations above the mean. This corresponds to approximately 2.6 standard deviations in a lognormal distribution and to a probability of 0.5 percent of deleting an observation.[8]

Extent and Consequences of Excluded Observations

These considerations generated twenty-three criteria on which establishment records might be excluded. They are listed in table 3.1. Because these rejection rules might have a substantial influence on the estimates of technical inefficiency, various tabulations were performed to assess the resulting rejection rates and their relationship to the measures of technical inefficiency. We analyzed the numbers of establishments rejected on each of these rules for 376 four-digit industries, which make up 84 percent of the four-digit industry population.[9] Before the application of rejection rules, the mean number of establishments available for analysis in each SIC industry was 168, with the range running from 18 to 2,191. The mean proportion of establishment records rejected for all reasons was 18 percent, with the rejected proportion running from 2.2 to 80.1 percent.

In column 1 of table 3.1 is reported the number of industries in which no establishments were rejected by each rule. Only two rules failed to result in one or more rejections in a large majority of the industries: capital expenditure exceeding twice the average of beginning- and end-of-year capital stocks and annual production worker hours exceeding 4,500. The pervasive incidence of rejections is reassuring in one sense because it suggests that the rejected establishment records are not clustered in a few industries for which quirks in the application of standard definitions could be causing wholesale but inappropriate exclusions.

Column 2 of table 3.1 provides another indicator of the relative importance of the various exclusion rules: the number of industries for which each criterion led to the rejection of more establishments than did any other. The clear front-runner was the requirement that average annual compensation per nonproduction worker fall between the values of $1,000 and $100,000. A distant second was the requirement that the plant report a strictly positive quantity of machinery in use. The prominence of questionable observations on the compensation of nonproduction workers raises some concern about the more sophisticated of our methods of measuring total labor input—the use of relative compensation of nonproduction and production workers as an index for converting their labor services into economically commensurable magnitudes.

Our rejection rules are not orthogonal in their effect, and establishments rejected on one criterion may frequently be rejected on another as well. The numerous rejection criteria listed in table 3.1 thus represent a proportionally smaller number of statistically independent bases for dropping establishment records from the analysis. In order to assess how much independence exists in the incidence of the rejection rules, a simple principal-components analysis was performed on the data matrix that consists of the number of records rejected on each criterion in each SIC industry. When the covariance method was used for estimating the principal components, the first eigenvector accounted for 96 percent of the total variance, and the second brought the cumulative proportion explained to 99 percent. Thus the rejection rules are far from being statistically independent in their incidence.

Several factors might indicate an influence of the rates of rejection on the subsequent estimates of technical inefficiency. One of these would be a significant relationship among SIC industries between rates of rejection and the numbers of good observations remaining.

Table 3.2
Percentile distributions of total numbers of establishment records, numbers
of records surviving rejection rules, and percentages of records rejected

Percentile	Rejection rate	Total observations	Good observations
100 max	80.0%	2,191	1,900
99	61.8	990	690
95	43.1	504	366
90	34.1	333	268
75	22.0	201	141
50	15.1	109	77
25	9.7	63	39
10	6.7	39	25
5	5.2	32	19
1	3.4	21	12
0 min	2.2	18	11
Total number of SIC industries	376	434	376

Table 3.2 provides some general background on percentile distributions over the SIC industries of the total number of establishment records, the number of records retained after application of the rejection rules, and the proportions of observations rejected. The median industry in terms of rejection rates lost 15.1 percent of its observations. When industries are ranked by number of observations, the median industry had 109. Ranked by observations valid for the analysis, the median is 77. A Spearman correlation coefficient was calculated between the total number of establishment records and the proportion rejected for each SIC industry. The correlation of -0.11 (significant at the 4 percent confidence level) implies that the lost observations were disproportionately concentrated in the industries with fewer plants. The correlation between the number of usable observations retained for each industry and its rejection rate was -0.25 (significant at the 0.1 percent level), confirming that rejection rates significantly influence the numbers of observations available for analysis.

We examined the ten industries that yielded rejection rates in excess of 50 percent to see what patterns might appear among them. The data are reported in table 3.3. The identities of these industries

Table 3.3
Industries with rates of rejection of establishment records exceeding 50 percent

SIC number	Industry	Establishments retained	Total establishments	Rate of rejection
2429	Special product sawmills, n.e.c.	31	64	51.6%
2371	Fur goods	12	28	57.1
2791	Typesetting	57	133	57.1
2741	Miscellaneous publishing	73	171	57.3
2299	Textile goods, n.e.c.	14	34	58.8
2335	Women's, misses', and juniors' dresses	330	835	60.5
2751	Commercial printing, letterpress and screen	296	768	61.5
2731	Books: publishing, publishing and printing	83	231	63.2
2721	Periodicals: publishing, publishing and printing	62	272	77.2
2411	Logging camps and contractors	157	787	80.1

cause no particular surprises. Half come from the two-digit group printing and publishing, which includes many establishments that report no production machinery and carry on no manufacturing activities in the conventional sense. Logging camps similarly fall outside the usual concept of a fixed-base manufacturing activity. The other industries subject to high rates of rejection are dominated by small-scale establishments in which errors in reporting may be proportionally larger and production activities that substantially violate one or more rejection criterion more common. Thus these industries seem to suffer from heavy rejection rates because of the natures of the activities that they undertake, not because of peculiarities in the collection or recording of data on these activities.

A final test of the effect of the rejection rules lies in their association with the calculated values for technical inefficiency (a question considered more extensively in chapter 6). Industries were divided into those for which we could compute positive variances for both the symmetrical and asymmetrical components of the composed-error term and those for which this condition was not satisfied (so that no measurement of technical inefficiency could be calculated). The mean overall rejection rate for observations was 17 percent for the former group of industries and 24 percent for the latter, and the difference between these means is statistically significant at the 1 percent confidence level. Thus the larger was the proportion of establishment records for an industry deleted by the editing rules, the less likely were the surviving observations to yield a result consistent with the basic assumptions of the methodology of stochastic frontier production functions.

A number of interpretations can be placed on that finding. One possible explanation is that the fewer observations available for analysis, the less likely is a satisfactory result to be obtained. The mean number of observations for well-behaved industries (139) was substantially larger than for those not yielding positive variances for both error-term components (49). Thus the effect of the editing rules may simply have been to reduce the available number of observations. Another interpretation is that the proportion of observations removed by the editing rules is an inverse indicator of the quality of data supplied by all establishments in the industry, including those not rejected. Still another possibility, the most disturbing one, is that the rejection rules are more likely than on a random basis to delete records for establishments that in fact are highly inefficient, removing just those observations that would provide the skewness to the composed residuals on which the methodology depends. Because an establishment's inability to report complete and accurate data could be correlated with its inability to carry out production activities with a high level of efficiency, such an association is not implausible.

4   Evaluation of Measures of Technical Inefficiency

We now evaluate the results of calculating stochastic frontier production functions according to the procedures described in chapters 2 and 3. This process requires more than simply summarizing the extent of technical inefficiency that has been revealed. Because the plausibility of key assumptions—about both the general methodology and our particular tactical decisions—is relatively untested for this novel methodology, the credibility of the results must be evaluated on whatever indicators fall to hand. Also we must determine the merits of the various transformations of the production function results that can be employed for comparing the technical efficiency of different industries. We take up this last question first and then summarize and evaluate the actual findings.

4.1 Measures of Technical Inefficiency

The direct output obtained when we compute the stochastic frontier production functions is estimates of the variance of the symmetrical (v) and asymmetrical (u) components of the overall variance. These can be normalized or otherwise stated in comparable form in several ways. The most elegant procedure is that proposed by Lee and Tyler (1978), who derived their measure of technical efficiency as the expected value of the ratio of actual to frontier output:

$$EFF = 2 * e^{\sigma^2(u)/2}\{1 - F(\sigma(u))\}.$$

where F is the standard normal distribution function. EFF depends only on the standard deviation and variance of the asymmetrical component of the component of the residuals, not on the mean level of productivity in the industry or the symmetrical component of the production function's variance.[1]

Some other investigators have expressed technical inefficiency as simply the shift in the intercept of the fitted production function that turns it into an estimated frontier (that is, the intercept shift) normalized by the mean of the dependent variable. This form has the disadvantage that the measure of inefficiency is not bounded from above. It can be made more satisfying, however, by expressing the intercept shift as a fraction of the estimated mean of the dependent variable measured on the frontier, approximated by the sum of the actual mean and the intercept shift:

$$ATI = \{(2/\pi)^{1/2}*\sigma(u)\}/(\bar{Y} + \{(2/\pi)^{1/2}*\sigma(u)\})$$

where $\bar{Y}$ is the mean of the dependent variable.

Two other candidates for the evaluation of technical inefficiency are available, both drawing on the composed-residual feature of the underlying model. In the standard derivation of the stochastic frontier production function, we encounter the term lambda (λ):

$$\lambda = \sigma(u)/\sigma(v).$$

The degree of asymmetry in the underlying residuals, which it measures, also has some claim to providing a normalized indicator of technical inefficiency. That a measure of estimated technical inefficiency decreases with the apparent randomness of the underlying production function relationship is surely an attractive property in that a large variance of random effects decreases our confidence that any asymmetry actually does represent technical inefficiency (Meeusen and van den Broeck 1977a). If we accept this proposition, then the skewness of the "raw" residuals that underlies the components of λ itself becomes a candidate for a measure of technical inefficiency that can be compared among industries.[2] Both λ and skewness (S) can be expressed in terms of the second ($U2$) and third ($U3$) moments of the residuals:

$$\lambda = \frac{\{(\pi/2)^{1/2}(\pi/(\pi-4))U3\}^{1/3}}{\{U2 - ((\pi-2)/\pi)((\pi/2)^{1/2}(\pi/(\pi-4)))U3^{2/3}\}^{1/2}}$$

while

$$S = -U3/U2^{3/2}.$$

Lambda (if allowed to take negative values) and skewness have a one-to-one correspondence over the range:

$-(\pi/(\pi-2))\{(\pi/2)^{1/2}(\pi/(\pi-4))\}^{-2/3} < S <$
$(\pi/(\pi-2))\{(\pi/2)^{1/2}(\pi/(\pi-4))\}^{-2/3}.$

Because this range runs from -0.9968 to 0.9968, the correspondence is practically complete. S has the property relative to λ of being comparable to a recognized measure of technical efficiency but also existing for those industries whose values of EFF, ATI, and λ cannot be estimated. Whether this property is desirable depends on the inference that one draws about the efficiency of an industry with a negative estimated variance of u. One interpretation holds that it exhibits no technical inefficiency, in which case the additional information contained in S is irrelevant. An alternative interpretation holds that it may exhibit some technical inefficiency that is obscured in the sample by the (opposite) skewness of the random effects captured by v. The greater is the positive skewness, however, the less likely is the existence of substantial technical inefficiency, so that the probable efficiency of the industry increases with S for values of $S > 0$.

The rationale for each of these measures has its desirable features. While EFF is the most attractive on purely formal grounds, the normalization for interindustry differences in either the mean dependent variable or the standard deviation of the random component (v) also has considerable appeal. The merit of S depends on empirical properties of the estimates of stochastic frontier production functions that are discussed below. In short, at this stage we are not prepared to rule out any of these measures, and it is attractive to use the similarity of the conclusions that they generate about interindustry differences in technical inefficiency as an indicator of the robustness of the results. It should be kept in mind that EFF and S are measures of efficiency, while ATI and λ are measures of inefficiency. In our analysis of interindustry differences, the sign predicted for a variable by a given hypothesis will differ between these two pairs of measures.

4.2 Patterns in Measures of Technical Inefficiency

Table 4.1 presents some important statistics describing the patterns of technical inefficiency indicated by the results. First, we were able to secure estimates of the extent of technical inefficiency for a maximum of 347 four-digit manufacturing industries using value added per unit of labor input as the dependent variable, 191 industries using gross output per employee (table 4.1a). The considerably larger yield for the former dependent variable deepens the doubts raised by our explora-

Table 4.1a
Means, standard deviations, and minimum and maximum values of measures of technical efficiency

Efficiency measure	Mean	Standard deviation	Minimum	Maximum	Number of observations
Based on value added					
EFF	0.275	0.173	0	0.941	344
ATI	0.502	0.156	0.057	0.841	334
λ	0.808	0.321	0.194	2.299	347
S	−0.096	0.088	−0.531	−0.002	345
Based on gross output					
EFF	0.630	0.152	0.253	0.975	183
ATI	0.054	0.031	0.005	0.177	179
λ	0.599	0.308	0.114	2.421	191
S	0.055	0.172	−2.283	0.119	185

tory work (chapter 3) concerning the quality of production function estimates with gross output as the dependent variable. The fits we obtained were by and large reasonable, with the average value of R^2 (corrected for degrees of freedom) equal to 0.26 for models based on value-added and 0.42 for those based on gross output. (The difference in fits probably reflects the simultaneous determination of output and material inputs.)

Overall Extent of Technical Inefficiency

The first question to put to these data is how much inefficiency exists on average in U.S. manufacturing industries. The mean values of the efficiency measures and other descriptive statistics appear in table 4.1a and the percentile distributions in table 4.1b. We focus on the measures EFF and ATI because they can be given direct interpretations. Alas, their agreement is less close than one might wish. Both indicate a low level of efficiency when the calculation is based on value added (27.5 and 50.2 percent, respectively). Both indicate higher levels of efficiency when gross output serves as the dependent variable (63.0 and 94.6 percent). Beyond that regularity, these mean values are spread so widely that they crush one's hopes of pronouncing confidently on overall extent of technical inefficiency. The other measures, λ and S, allow no such direct interpretations, but they

Table 4.1b
Percentile values for efficiency measures

Measure	Percentiles						
	0	10	25	50	75	90	100
EFF(VA)	0.00	0.11	0.15	0.23	0.37	0.51	0.94
EFF(GO)	0.25	0.43	0.51	0.64	0.73	0.84	0.98
ATI(VA)	0.06	0.28	0.39	0.51	0.62	0.71	0.84
ATI(GO)	0.00	0.02	0.03	0.05	0.07	0.10	0.18
λ(VA)	0.19	0.47	0.60	0.75	0.97	1.22	2.30
λ(GO)	0.11	0.28	0.39	0.55	0.70	1.02	2.42
S(VA)	−0.53	−0.18	−0.11	−0.05	−0.02	0.04	0.32
S(GO)	−2.28	−0.06	−0.03	0.01	0.04	0.09	0.39

agree with EFF and ATI in indicating more inefficiency when value added serves as the dependent variable.[3]

On the evidence assembled so far, EFF based on value added has a substantial claim to the status of preferred measure of efficiency. Therefore we were somewhat dismayed to observe that it indicates a mean level of efficiency rather lower than those reported in previous studies, which mostly have fallen in the range of 0.6 to 0.9 (as does EFF based on gross output). To probe this pattern (and for various other diagnostic uses in this chapter), we examined the range for each industry between the maximum and minimum values for individual plants of the dependent variables (value-added per unit of labor input; gross output per employee). For establishments in each industry, we calculated the ratio of the maximum to the minimum observation, denoted MMVA and MMGO, respectively. They allowed us to establish that the low mean value of EFF based on value added is due to the form chosen for the dependent variable. The mean value of MMVA is much higher than that of MMGO. That is because some plants exist with barely positive levels of value added (plants with negative value added were excluded from the analysis). Gross output is not subject to the same incidence of marginally positive values and accordingly yields much higher mean values of EFF. This discovery indicates that the low mean EFF based on value added should not be taken at its face value and also leaves credible the claim of this measure to provide a good indication of interindustry differences in efficiency.

We can indeed turn to the evidence in table 4.1 on the interindustry distribution of efficiency levels. The standard deviations shown in table 4.1a and the distributions in table 4.1b hold some interest. The standard deviation of EFF based on value added exceeds that for EFF based on gross output, and table 4.1b shows this to be due to a piling up of low values of the former (consistent with the observation about MMVA). Skewness (S) works in the opposite way, with its standard deviation doubled for the computation based on gross output, and the pattern due to an elongated tail of low-efficiency observations when based on gross output. The pattern for ATI resembles that for EFF, keeping in mind that ATI is a measure of inefficiency, and so its elongated upper tail in the value-added case corresponds to EFF's elongated lower tail. These comparisons confirm that the efficiency measures exhibit patterns differing enough that, as dependent variables, their interindustry differences might appear to have quite different statistical explanations.

Similarity of Industries' Rankings

If the measures give divergent signals about average levels of inefficiency, how similar are their rankings of industries? Table 4.2 reports Spearman correlation coefficients among the four measures (with levels of statistical significance in parentheses). The correlation matrix also includes the number of observations of individual establishments from which each industry's frontier production function was estimated. Despite differing means and distributions, nearly all pairs of measures exhibit highly significant correlations with each other. For λ and S that is no surprise, for reasons explained in section 4.1. However, high correlations between other pairs are not due to the construction of the measures. The correlations between EFF and ATI, the variables with the best pedigrees, are not only highly significant but also high enough in absolute value that exogenous variables will almost surely exert similar effects on them. For measures based on value added, each pair is significantly correlated at the 0.1 percent level of confidence. For gross output, however, some correlations are insignificant. Indeed every correlation except for EFF and ATI is considerably lower for gross output than for value added.

The correlations in table 4.2 suggest two conclusions. First, the gross differences in mean efficiency levels suggested in table 4.1 do not translate into similarly large differences in industries' rankings by

Table 4.2
Correlations (Spearman) between measures of technical inefficiency and with number of establishments in each industry utilized to estimate frontier production function

	EFF	ATI	λ	S	Number of observations
Based on value added					
EFF	1.000	−0.975	−0.490	0.480	−0.695
		(0.0001)	(0.0001)	(0.0001)	(0.0001)
ATI		1.000	0.528	−0.518	0.671
			(0.0001)	(0.0001)	(0.0001)
λ			1.000	−0.994	−0.103
				(0.0001)	(0.0553)
S				1.000	0.116
					(0.0312)
Number of observations					1.000
Based on gross output					
EFF	1.000	−0.997	−0.048	0.073	−0.655
		(0.0001)	(0.522)	(0.323)	(0.0001)
ATI		1.000	0.105	−0.101	0.629
			(0.162)	(0.179)	(0.0001)
λ			1.000	−0.970	−0.599
				(0.0001)	(0.0001)
S				1.000	0.531
					(0.0001)
Number of observations					1.000

Note: Significance probabilities appear in parentheses.

the different measures. On the contrary, they are highly similar, especially those based on value added. This finding supports our basic strategy of emphasizing the inferences that can be drawn from interindustry differences. Second, the evidence of the lower quality of measures based on gross output is increased.

Finally, consider the correlations with the number of plants in each industry (last column of table 4.2). Taken literally, they imply that efficiency decreases significantly with the number of plants (significant at 5 percent and usually much higher, for each measure). Because the number of plants is closely related to the number of firms and, generally, competitive conditions in each industry, this pattern is both important and surprising. We consider it closely in section 4.3.

Table 4.3
Comparison of estimates of technical efficiency in 162 industries for which
stochastic frontier production function could be estimated with both value
added (VA) and gross output (GO) as dependent variables

Variable		Mean	Standard deviation	Coefficient of variation	Minimum value	Maximum value
EFF:	VA	0.278	0.155	0.557	0.000	0.877
	GO	0.601	0.134	0.223	0.253	0.894
ATI:	VA	0.486	0.153	0.314	0.057	0.772
	GO	0.057	0.030	0.526	0.011	0.177
λ:	VA	0.886	0.351	0.396	0.314	2.299
	GO	0.530	0.215	0.407	0.114	1.404
S:	VA	−0.117	0.101	n.a.	−0.531	−0.006
	GO	−0.037	0.039	n.a.	−0.268	0.014

Note: n.a. = not applicable.

This evaluation of the production functions estimated from value added and gross output can be pursued further by examining the subset of industries for which both variables yield estimates of technical inefficiency. Summary statistics describing the measures for these 159 industries appear in table 4.3. For this group of industries, all four measures again point to more inefficiency when value added serves as the dependent variable. We also show coefficients of variation, which for *EFF* (but not *ATI* or λ) differ greatly between the data based on value added and gross output.

Differences between Industries with and without Estimates

We have so far put aside industries for which *EFF*, *ATI*, and λ could not be estimated. However, the differences between those industries and the ones covered in table 4.1 call for some consideration. The stochastic frontier production function model implies that industries for which *EFF*, *ATI*, and λ cannot be estimated (for which $S > 0$) should be without significant technical inefficiency. Although we treat the structural differences between industries with and without estimates of inefficiency as only the most preliminary test of the determinants of technical efficiency, we nonetheless need to consider how the two sets differ as a check on the plausibility of the basic model.

Table 4.4
Relationship between ability to estimate technical inefficiency for an industry
and ratio of maximum to minimum values of dependent variable in frontier
production function

	Number (and percentage) of industries		
Ratio of maximum to minimum value, net output per unit labor input	Industries with no estimate of technical ineffiency (NA industries)	Industries with estimated technical inefficiency (TI industries)	Total
0–15	50 (54.9%)	92 (26.8%)	142
15–50	28 (30.8%)	116 (33.8%)	144
50 or more	13 (14.3%)	135 (39.4%)	148
Total	91	343	434

One check is provided by means of the ratios of the maximum to minimum values of the dependent variables, *MMVA* and *MMGO*. If industries for which the technical-efficiency measures could not be calculated (hereafter NA industries) are largely free of technical inefficiency, we would expect them to exhibit lower values of *MMVA* and *MMGO* than industries yielding estimates of technical inefficiency (TI industries). Table 4.4 shows that this is the case. Fifty-five percent of the NA industries have ratios of 15 or less, only half that proportion for the TI industries; four-tenths of the TI industries show ratios over 50 but only one-seventh of the NA industries. In a chi-square test, the pattern shown in table 4.4 proves significant at the 0.1 percent level.[4]

Some other comparisons can be made in the same spirit. Consider the goodness of fit of the production functions estimated for the two groups of industries. We would expect the presence of substantial technical inefficiency to reduce the precision with which the function can be estimated and produce lower values of the coefficient of determination (corrected for degrees of freedom). The mean of these coefficients is 0.24 for 295 TI industries and 0.35 for 66 NA industries. The difference between the two means is significant at the 1 percent level, so the hypothesis is confirmed.

Another comparison turns on the quality of industry definitions and the null hypothesis that technical inefficiency might be an artifact of poorly defined industries. We can distinguish between product shipments (total shipments of products classified to the industry) and industry shipments (total shipments by establishments classified to the industry). Their divergence reflects the degree to which plants classified to the industry ship secondary products classified to other industries, as well as the degree to which shipments of this industry's product emanate as secondary products from plants classified to other industries. We formed the ratio [1 − (product shipments)/ (industry shipments)]. The larger is its absolute value, the more heterogeneous are the activities of the establishments shipping products classified to the industry. When we calculated the mean values for NA and TI industries, we obtained values of 0.134 and 0.112, respectively. The putatively efficient industries are less homogeneous. Thus it seems unlikely that our measures of technical inefficiency are strongly affected by data that have been polluted by diversification.[5]

The relative sizes of the NA and TI populations are one point of reference. Of the 433 industries with enough observations for frontier production functions to be estimated, only 76 failed to yield estimates of λ on the basis of value added as the dependent variable. Is it generally plausible that four-fifths of U.S. manufacturing industries would exhibit some technical inefficiency and the remainder none that we could detect? We would say yes on the basis of a large but diffuse body of prior empirical evidence, but that answer can admittedly be defended only as a general judgment. Consider the null hypothesis that suggests itself when the fraction of TI industries falls to one-half or less (as it does with the functions based on gross output and in previous studies for other countries, such as Corbo and de Melo 1983). The null hypothesis holds that the composed residuals model fundamentally fails to capture any systematic evidence of technical inefficiency. Instead the purely random residuals in the production function, by assumption normally distributed in the population, may with equal probability be positively or negatively skewed in the sample comprising the establishments in a particular industry. Then half the industries for which stochastic frontier production functions are calculated would on average appear to harbor some technical inefficiency, while the positively skewed half would not. The 80 percent yield in the production functions based on value added carries considerable weight against this null hypothesis, even if the less satisfactory results based on gross output do not reject it.[6]

Another test that can be applied addresses the effect of the data-editing rules described in chapter 3. To take an extreme case, suppose that the underlying data exhibit a high content of errors but one that varies systematically from industry to industry. The TI industries might be "bad data" industries, with numerous erroneous data points that just missed being excluded by our editing rules, so that technical inefficiency might be inferred from nothing more than unevenly distributed bad data. If that were the case, the proportion of observations in the Census files excluded by the editing rules should be larger in the TI than the NA industries.[7] In fact the mean difference runs the other way: 24.6 percent excluded in the mean NA industry and 16.9 percent in the mean TI industry. The difference between these means is significant at the 1 percent level. Therefore we reject the null hypothesis that the results might strongly reflect interindustry differences in data quality.[8]

Our last experiment was to employ the variables used for testing hypotheses about interindustry differences in efficiency in a purely inductive way to test for associations with *MMVA*. A stepwise regression program was allowed to select the most significant regressors from each of several groups. The first group is a class of variables that we consider (see chapters 5 and 6) the primary determinants of technical efficiency. Three of the variables that surfaced as the strongest influences on *MMVA* are measures of the heterogeneity of the manufacturing industries defined in the SIC: the proportion of shipments from establishments classified to the industry made by establishments belonging to firms classified to other industries (the "enterprise coverage ratio"); the proportion of shipments from establishments belonging to firms classified to the industry made by their establishments classified to other industries (the "enterprise specialization ratio"); and the proportion of the industry's value of shipments accounted for by inputs purchased from primary sectors. Another group of substantive variables were those embodying secondary hypotheses in the cross-section analysis of chapters 5 and 6. In this case two of the five most significant influences were measures of the vintage dispersion of the industry's capital stock, another source of heterogeneity.

Do our measures of technical efficiency convey substantial information about that phenomenon? In this subsection tests are reported of several corollaries that tend to validate the measures. One group supports the corollary of the research methodology that industries for which technical efficiency cannot be measured in fact exhibit little inefficiency. Other tests indicate that the quality of data provided by establishments in the TI industries is no worse (better, apparently) than that supplied by NA industries. These two findings point in somewhat different directions regarding one's interpretation of the NA industries. However, those are not our concern, and both conclusions do tend to validate the measurement of technical efficiency.

4.3 Relation between Technical Efficiency and Number of Observations

We noticed highly significant correlations in table 4.2 between the measures of efficiency and the numbers of establishments used to estimate the frontier production functions. Taken substantively at face value, these correlations imply that large-numbers, competitive industries exhibit high levels of inefficiency—a conclusion that flies in the face of a great deal of economic theory and empirical evidence. When we analyzed ratios of establishments' maximum to minimum values for the dependent variables ($MMVA$ and $MMGO$), these proved to be highly correlated with the number of establishment records used to estimate each production function (0.558 for $MMVA$, 0.502 for $MMGO$, each significant at the 0.1 percent level). In addition $MMVA$ and $MMGO$ are highly correlated with the measures of technical efficiency,[9] as well as being significantly higher in industries that apparently exhibit some technical inefficiency (TI industries).[10]

Order Statistics

This evidence led us to recognize that a purely statistical factor exists that is sufficient to explain the relationship. We first provide a simple demonstration to support the intuition that apparent technical efficiency will be associated with the number of observations drawn from a distribution because the extreme values will increase with the number of observations. Assume an industry consisting of n establishments, each using identical quantities of inputs. X_i is the output of the ith establishment, and the X_i are arrayed from the smallest (X_1) to the largest (X_n). Consider technical efficiency to be a nonstochastic concept, with the efficiency of the ith establishment defined as $TE_i = X_i/X_n$. Then we can derive mean technical efficiency for the industry as follows:

$$E(TE) = (1/n) \sum_i (X_i/X_n)$$
$$= (1/n)(1/X_n) \sum_i X_i.$$

Let $U \equiv E(X_i)$. Then:

$E(TE) = (1/n)(1/X_n)(n*U) = U/X_n = f(U,n)$.

That is, a deterministic frontier defined in this way would depend on the mean and the highest observed value of the distribution. If the maximum value increases with the number of observations sampled, so will the apparent extent of technical inefficiency.[11]

The theory of order statistics establishes just this relationship between the extreme values of observations in a sample, or the range of observations in an ordered sample, and the number of observations drawn. The intuition is that when a very small sample (say, two) has been drawn from a normal distribution, the probability that the next observation will lie outside the range running from the smallest to the largest already drawn is very high; as the sample size increases, the chance that the next drawing will enlarge the observed range declines monotonically. For example, Owen (1962, p. 151) provided the following relation between the size of the sample drawn from a $N(0,1)$ distribution and the expected value of the largest observation to have been drawn (X_n):

Sample size	$E(X_n)$
20	1.87
30	2.04
40	2.16
50	2.25

For symmetric $(0,1)$ populations, Kendall and Stuart (1969, p. 340) derived the following expression for the expected value of the range between minimum and maximum values $[E(R)]$ as a function of sample size:

$0 \le E(R) \le (n + 0.5)^{0.5}$.

Similarly, Kendall and Stuart (1969, p. 327) provided an expression for the standard error of the midpoint of a range $[= 0.5(X_1 + X_n)]$. It is an increasing function of the standard error of the mean of the distribution. Furthermore, it goes to infinity as the sample size goes to infinity, indicating that asymptotic properties will not limit the dependence of apparent technical inefficiency on the number of observations as that number increases.

Table 4.5a
Logarithmic regressions of technical efficiency on number of plants from which frontier production function was estimated

Dependent variable	Constant	Coefficient of ln (number of plants)	$\bar{R}^2$	F	Number of industries
EFF (VA)	0.561	−0.435	0.41	223	316
	(4.16)	(2.24)			
ATI (VA)	−2.161	0.304	0.38	194	316
	(21.43)	(8.99)			
EEF (GO)	0.433	−0.216	0.44	141	178
	(5.39)	(15.56)			
ATI (GO)	−5.415	0.534	0.42	132	178
	(26.43)	(0.73)			

Note: t-statistics appear in parentheses. Those for the coefficient of the logarithm of the number of establishments have been calculated on the null hypothesis that the coefficient equals 0.5.

Empirical Evidence

Each of these formulations of the relationship between extreme values and number of observations implies that the range of extreme values increases with something close to the square root of the number of observations. If the relationship between technical efficiency and the number of observations in our sample is close to this form, we cannot reject the hypothesis that the dependence of technical efficiency on the number of observations is a purely statistical phenomenon. We regressed the logarithms of EFF and ATI in turn on the number of plants from which each stochastic frontier production function was estimated, obtaining the result reported in table 4.5a. The t-statistics shown there test the hypothesis that the coefficient of the logarithm of the number of observations differs from 0.5 (for ATI) or −0.5 (for EFF). Two of the estimated coefficients lie rather close to the value indicated by this analysis based on order statistics. However, only one of them is not statistically different from 0.5. In evaluating this conclusion, one should note the significant intercepts in the equations, which tend to tilt the slope coefficients in each case away from 0.5 in the observed direction. The number of observations explains around 40 percent of the variance of EFF or ATI for the measures based on value-added.

Table 4.5b
Technical efficiency levels predicted from table 4.5a as a function of number of plants

Number of plants	Measure of technical efficiency			
	EFF (VA)	ATI (VA)	EFF (GO)	ATI (GO)
10	0.643	0.232	0.937	0.015
20	0.476	0.286	0.806	0.022
40	0.352	0.354	0.694	0.032
80	0.260	0.437	0.598	0.046
160	0.192	0.539	0.515	0.067
320	0.142	0.665	0.443	0.097
640	0.105	0.821	0.381	0.140
1,280	0.078	1.010	0.328	0.203

The magnitude of the relation between technical efficiency and the number of observations is demonstrated in table 4.5b, in which we report values predicted from the regressions in table 4.5a. As they show, unless the statistical interpretation offered here is accepted, one's evaluation of the substantive determinants of technical efficiency will surely be dominated by its decrease with the number of units observed.

The variable $MMVA$ provides one test of the order-statistics interpretation. That interpretation implies that the number of observations should be positively correlated with $MMVA$ to similar degrees for NA and TI industries. That is, in whichever direction the production function residuals prove to be skewed, that skewness should increase with the number of observations entering into the estimation. Conversely a correlation found in the TI industries only would suggest a behavioral interpretation—that inefficiency does increase with the number of units in the industry. The correlation is lower for the NA industries (0.37) than for the TI industries (0.57) but highly signficant in both cases. The high and significant values of both coefficients support the order-statistics interpretation, but the greater magnitude of the one for the TI industries is surely cautionary.

Overall the evidence lends support to the order-statistics hypothesis although not to the point of assuaging all concern that a negative behavioral relation may exist between efficiency and the number of units. For the purpose of analyzing the theoretically founded behavioral determinants of technical efficiency, we shall provisionally accept the order-statistics interpretation. In the statistical analysis of the interindustry determinants of technical efficiency (chapter 6), we shall remove its influence by including the square root of the number of observations as a regressor.

4.4 Summary

At this point we can summarize the empirical findings embodied in stochastic frontier productions estimated for a maximum of 347 U.S. manufacturing industries. The crucial statistic obtained from the estimated production function is the standard deviation of the one-sided error component that is assumed to represent technical efficiency. In order to interpret that statistic and make it comparable among industries, some normalization is required. We prefer the Lee-Tyler measure, expected technical efficiency; however, competing normalizations (by the mean of the dependent variable; by the standard deviation of the symmetrical component of the residuals) have their attractions.

The correlations among these alternative measures are high but not so high as to preclude different results when they serve as dependent variables in cross section; all are kept in play. The correlations are lower among efficiency estimates based on gross output rather than value added as the dependent variable; indeed the estimates based on gross output appear inferior on a number of tests and are largely put aside for the balance of the study.

Although the correlations among these technical-efficiency measures are high, their mean values differ greatly. Means are also strongly affected by the choice between value added and gross output as a dependent variable in the production function—a pattern that has an economic explanation. To the question, "How inefficient is U.S. industry?" we must reply: "A little or a lot, depending on how you measure it." Fortunately this pattern of high correlations but dispersed means supports our original intention to focus on the determinants of interindustry variance.

Technical inefficiency cannot be estimated for some industries because the composed residuals are skewed in the wrong direction. For the method plausibly to capture technical inefficiency, a generous majority of industries should indicate the presence of some inefficiency. With value added as the dependent variable, about four-fifths of industries for which production functions could be estimated do reveal some inefficiency. Several simple tests support the hypothesis that "no estimate" industries are in fact efficient. They have smaller total ranges between the minimum and maximum values of the dependent variable in the production function. They are less affected by diversification (leading to increased random noise and close calls as to whether plants should be assigned to one or another industry). We also tested whether the underlying Census data for industries inferred to be technically inefficient could be deemed of lower quality than data for efficient industries. In fact, the opposite is the case: the fits of the production functions are on average rather better for the inefficient industries. Also the editing rules we employed to delete apparently faulty plant records before estimating the frontier production functions discarded more observations for the "no estimate" industries than for those yielding estimates of technical inefficiency. That finding supports some confidence that the estimated values of technical efficiency were not strongly influenced by the editing rules.

A major puzzle that surfaced in this preliminary assessment of the technical-efficiency estimates is a highly significant negative correlation between estimated efficiency and the number of plant observations used to estimate the production function. Taken as an economic relation, this pattern would upend the strongly held prior belief that competition disciplines or eliminates inefficient producers. We developed an explanation for this correlation based on order statistics and performed several statistical tests of the explanation; they provide substantial but not complete support. While we accept the order-statistics explanation, the phenomenon must be recognized as a qualification on any finding about competition and efficiency based on the number of competitors present in the market.

5

Interindustry Determinants of Technical Inefficiency

5.1 Introduction

This chapter sets out the hypotheses to be tested about the differences among industries in the technical efficiency of their plants. It is concerned with the analytical background of these hypotheses, the relevant empirical evidence from previous studies, and the best possible specification of independent variables from the available statistical resources.

Bases for Modeling Technical Inefficiency

Because the existence and nature of technical inefficiency have been quite controversial in the literature of industrial economics, we give brief attention to the conditions under which economic analysis can consistently identify normatively objectionable sources of technical inefficiency. The doubters (Stigler 1976) have urged that the assumptions that businesses maximize profits, that individuals maximize utility, or both together somehow preclude the use of economic analysis to identify sources of technical inefficiency (some economists would say that they preclude technical inefficiency itself). However, at least four sets of circumstances are consistent with technical inefficiency persisting in a cogently described economic equilibrium:

1. The firm consists of a coalition of workers and other factors of production joined in long-term but incomplete contracts. Even if these contracts are "perfect" (that is, Pareto optimal) ex ante, they may fail ex post through shirking or other opportunistic behavior by some members of the coalition; with the shirking anticipated, they are second best at the outset. This approach embraces both the Carnegie school's concern with lateral contracts among functional special-

ists and the theory of imperfect vertical contracts in the literature on transactions between principals and agents. It includes both the non-maximizing approaches of the Carnegie group and Leibenstein (1976) and the utility-maximization models in the principal-agent literature.

2. Information about the most efficient ways to do things may be costly and may diffuse only slowly and imperfectly through an industry, so that some decision units are inefficient because failures in the market for information have deprived them of the knowledge needed to improve their ways. This approach is implicit in search theory and in empirical approaches to the diffusion of innovation.

3. Where competition is imperfect and firms recognize their mutual competitive dependence, considerations of oligopolistic strategy may affect the decisions that some firms make about their scales of operation or their levels of certain inputs or activities, so that what is (or may be) profit maximizing to the individual firm becomes technically inefficient from the viewpoint of society. This behavior was modeled by Fershtman and Muller (1986) following many empirical tests on sales promotion outlays, research expenditures, and the incidence of excess capacity.

4. In some sectors regulatory constraints produce inefficiency by restricting entry of competitors, constraining the activities or market territories of incumbents, and in various other ways that have been identified in studies of the effects of regulation on particular industries (e.g., Bruning and Olson 1982). Despite the importance of regulation for the efficiency of some sectors, it will not be pursued as a determinant of interindustry differences in efficiency because it is impractical to quantify the differences in regulation that exist among typical manufacturing industries.

These bases for inefficiency are considered more fully below as we seek statistical embodiments for them. Besides the normatively significant bases for technical inefficiency suggested by these conditions, we shall control for numerous other factors that may explain the technical inefficiency we measure and contribute to our understanding of market processes but hold no such direct implications for public policy.

Limitations of Measurement

Before proceeding to the hypotheses and explanatory variables, we should notice certain properties of the measures of technical inefficiency that affect which distorting influences can and cannot be detected:

1. They will not directly reflect the prevalence of plants that operate at inefficiently small scales but minimize costs at those scales. The production function form employed allows for variations in productivity with scale. A plant that is the wrong size to attain maximum productivity is therefore counted as inefficient only to the extent that it falls short of the estimated productivity attainable in a plant of its own scale.

2. The methodology of frontier production functions stresses the distinction between inefficiency due to quantities of all inputs that are excessive, given the output, and to inefficient combinations of inputs (that would be efficient for some other set of input prices). In this study most input prices are unobserved, so this distinction cannot be implemented. While in principle only technical efficiency is measured, the diverse input choice of an industry's plants may enter into the measure. The research strategy permits testing some relationships between technical efficiency and the diversity of units' input choices.[1]

3. The methodology depends fundamentally on differences in efficiency levels among units classified to an industry, so that factors causing units to be uniformly inefficient will not be detected. Suppose, for example, that a group of oligopolists maintains a price-fixing agreement that induces each of them to maintain the same amount of excess capacity.[2] Although the costs of producing the industry's actual output level will exceed the socially necessary minimum, member firms will appear to attain the same productivity frontier.

Our measures should reveal all aspects of technical inefficiency that remain after these deletions. In proposing hypotheses about factors determining the dispersion of plants' efficiency levels relative to the efficiency frontier, we shall distinguish them from hypotheses that might relate to the position of the frontier itself, to the efficiency of the scales of observed production units, or other aspects of efficiency beyond the reach of our measures.

5.2 Competitive Conditions

The relationship of competitive conditions to technical inefficiency has a number of strands, which in turn suggest diverse ways of measuring competitive conditions in the industry. The level of technical efficiency has been linked to an industry's competitive conditions in several ways that are closely related to the theoretical bases for technical inefficiency .

Hypotheses about Competitive Conditions

1. Expansion of slack within the plant or firm.
As the Carnegie-Mellon school suggests, the firm may be viewed as a coalition of specialized factors of production that strike lateral contracts reflecting their individual preferences and interests in policies to be followed by the firm (as well as their demands for pecuniary compensation). Rewarding the coalition's members in nonpecuniary forms (slack, policy side payments) does not itself necessarily produce inefficiency. However, members of the coalition have an incentive to increase the benefits that they appropriate to themselves if a "surplus" is available to the participants. This ex post opportunism is a source of technical inefficiency. External competition limits this opportunism because the presence of efficient rivals (or the threat of their entry) constrains the amount of slack a firm's participants can absorb and the technical inefficiency they can generate without making the coalition infeasible.[3] This proposition is more easily accepted as an intuition than proved formally. Hart (1983) did demonstrate a specific mechanism whereby market competition from efficient firms imposes efficiency on competitors subject to second-best principal-agent contracts, but it is very specialized and not robust (Scharfstein 1988). The real theoretical question may be what conditions ensure the presence of some efficient firms. If some competitors can be inefficient, why can't they all? If one accepts organizational equilibria with areas of inertia, as Leibenstein proposed, whence come organizations that are not stuck on such "flat spots"? On the other hand, it takes only a constant (nonzero) probability that a randomly drawn firm will be efficient to make the probability that an efficient competitor is present increase with the number of competitors.

2. Economic experiment and information flows.
In seeking productivity improvements and reacting to economic changes, the individuals firms and plants in an industry continually perform experiments. Technical efficiency for the industry as a whole is higher the more numerous are the experimenters and the more freely does information on the experimental outcomes flow through

the industry. This consideration implies that the presence of numerous competitors should increase technical efficiency by providing more experimenters. It suggests that large numbers of participants favor the diffusion of information in the sense that the more parties know the outcome of a given experiment, the more likely is it to leak and become public knowledge (Winter 1971; Carlsson 1972; McCain 1975). What this argument predicts about measured technical efficiency is not entirely clear. Competitive experimentation might lead over time to a higher average level of efficiency, but it also is consistent with more diversity of units' productivity levels along the way.

3. Imperfect competition and resource use.
The recognition of mutual dependence among rival firms may lead them to make business decisions that commit resources for the purpose of deterring or influencing rivals or maintaining understandings with them. Firms may enter the industry at inefficient scales of operation or otherwise make inefficient commitments of resources because of opportunities to benefit from an umbrella provided by mutually dependent pricing.[4] Many economists have suggested that discretionary expenditures such as advertising are affected by the presence of incomplete oligopolistic bargains, and these may include such explicit forms of technical inefficiency as maintaining excess capacity to take advantage of inflated price-cost margins or to threaten rivals with retaliation for competitive moves. These resource commitments will not turn up as technical inefficiency if they are undertaken uniformly by all parties to incomplete collusive arrangements. However, diverse sorts of differences among competitors (such as market share) will render their incentives dissimilar (Porter 1979).

Previous empirical research (mostly on countries other than the United States) has obtained mixed results on the hypothesized influence of competition. Downie (1958) found that technical efficiency in British manufacturing industries was worsened by the conjunction of high seller concentration and the prevalence of collusive agreements. Carlsson (1972) concluded that in Sweden the more concentrated industries are efficient; he attributed this unexpected result to the joint effect of scale economies and the small size of the Swedish industrial sector. Research on long-run excess capacity—a specific form of technical inefficiency—has associated its prevalence with moderate seller concentration and (implicitly) the presence of incomplete oligopolistic understandings.[5] Finally, potential rivals and ease of entry increase effective competition, and low entry barriers make the emergence of efficient and/or noncooperating rivals more likely and threaten the survival of inefficiency incumbents. We have some statistical evidence (Fraser and Rose 1972) that entry increases the technical efficiency of incumbents in concentrated markets, as well as more casual but dramatic evidence from the reactions of U.S. manufacturing industries (e.g., Lawrence and Dyer 1983) to the pressure of import competition.

Variables Used

The basic variable to indicate the competitive conditions in an industry, in response to these hypotheses, is the standard four-firm seller concentration ratio:

$CONC$ = percentage of shipments accounted for by four largest firms, 1977.

It is not ideal because empirical evidence indicates that the inequality of shares among the leading four firms wields an influence on competition but is not reflected in the concentration ratio. Still, that ratio is highly correlated with any of the conceptually superior but not readily available measures. One the first two sets of considerations outlined above, it should have a negative effect on technical efficiency. The third set, however, suggests that the maximum inefficiency may occur in moderately concentrated industries.[6] We can also make use of:

$C4AJ$ = $CONC$ adjusted for international competition, regional submarkets, and imperfections in market definitions (Weiss and Pascoe 1986).

The Weiss-Pascoe measure $C4AJ$ improves on $CONC$ as a measure of potential departures from competition; however, the use of $CONC$ remains appropriate for this study because other hypotheses will be introduced that independently link these adjustments to technical efficiency.

Although the seller concentration ratio provides the most basic measure of competitive conditions, several other of their aspects should be taken into account. Because theory and empirical evidence associate inefficiency with collusion on price, the number of indictments previously brought against members of each industry for maintaining anticompetitive agreements was obtained:

$VIOL$ = number of indictments for violations of Sherman Act Section 1 brought against firms classified to the industry, 1958–1977.

The leverage of $VIOL$ will be limited because it is greater than zero for only forty-six industries. We assume that indictments were positively correlated with violations that actually occurred but that the subsequent prosecutions (if any) attenuated the industry's propensity to collude without destroying it. Clearly the variable could fail either if this smoke-equals-fire assumption is wrong or if prosecutions on average promptly repaired all adverse effects of the collusion.[7] The effectiveness or sustainability of collusion may depend on the level of concentration, a possibility that is readily tested statistically.

Exposure to international trade is an important force imposing competition on domestic producers. It seemed imperative to isolate its influence rather than simply adjust $CONC$ as in previous research on allocative efficiency.[8] The existence of opportunities for American producers to sell in export markets is also generally thought to make a U.S. industry more competitive than it would be if the same producers sold only in the U.S. market. The reasoning is that world markets outside the United States bring American producers into competition with a large, shifting, and unfamiliar group of foreign rivals. Therefore export markets in the large are never less competitive than is the U.S. domestic market though individual overseas markets may of course be noncompetitive for their own domestic producers). The variables used are:

MS = imports divided by industry shipments plus imports, averaged over 1972–1976.

XS = exports divided by industry shipments, averaged over 1972–1976.

The power of our tests of the influence of these variables, especially MS, will be limited by missing observations (because for many industries trade and production data cannot be cleanly matched).

MS should wield a positive influence on technical efficiency, as should XS if indeed it exerts a procompetitive force. However, previous research on exporting activities (Auquier 1980; Caves 1986) indicated that exporting activity is spread quite unevenly among the typical exporting industry's production units, apparently due to fixed distribution or related costs that are large relative to those entailed for domestic sales. As a consequence, large production units are more likely to export than small ones, and small units that export are likely to export large proportions of their outputs. Such a pattern will expand the variance of margins and could well raise the revenue-production frontier and increase apparent technical inefficiency (Chen and Tang 1987). Hence, a two-tail test should be used on the coefficient of XS.

Just as import competition is expected to improve technical efficiency, so should tariff protection worsen it. Carlsson (1972) found technical inefficiency in Swedish industries to be significantly increased by tariffs and apparently reduced by exposure to international trade.[9] A problem arises, however, whether tariffs and other restrictions on imports directly affect efficiency. If trade barriers simply keep out imports, their effect is only indirect. That is, more imports promote greater technical efficiency, and higher tariffs permit fewer imports. However, tariffs may also directly affect technical efficiency by giving a signal to producers that policymakers stand ready to mitigate competitive pressures affecting an industry by virtue of having done so before.[10] The downside risk to firms that operate inefficiently is thereby reduced. Reluctantly, because of the lack of satisfactory measures at the four-digit SIC level of effective protection and the incidence of nontariff barriers, we put this consideration aside and assume that only operative import competition matters.

5.3 Product Differentiation and Heterogeneity

Rival sellers in an industry can appear to differ in efficiency for a number of reasons associated with qualitative differences in the inputs they utilize and differences in buyers' willingness to pay for the outputs they offer. Such differences in efficiency or revenue productivity have no simple normative interpretations, but it remains important to control for any effect they exert on the measured extent of technical inefficiency.

Effect on Technical Efficiency

Assume that each of an industry's sellers offers a uniquely differentiated product and that some serve larger markets or buyers with greater willingness to pay. If the rents obtained by successful sellers cannot be competed away, they will appear to be more efficient technically than sellers who are less successful or serve small niches of the market that (due to scale economies) allow them to earn only normal profits. Therefore the extent of structural product differentiation in an industry should increase the variance of the gross profit rates of its firms. Whether that greater variance inflates apparent technical inefficiency, however, is not clear. Without an explicit model of the brand structure of a market, we can say only that it increases the symmetrical (v) component of the composed error term in the stochastic frontier production function. In a particular case, it might either augment the skewness that indicates apparent technical inefficiency or foster the opposite-sign skewness that makes an industry appear to be without inefficiency (for example, where most brands earn normal profits but a few obtain substantial rents). Nonetheless, both Carlsson (1972) and Corbo and de Melo (1983) found technical efficiency lower in industries with more heterogeneous products.

Empirical research on industrial economics has tended to settle for the industry's advertising intensity (advertising-sales ratio) as a measure of the differentiation of its product. Advertising by producers may be a sufficient indicator for differentiation, but it does not address the underlying conditions that account for product differentiation. We need to identify these conditions in order to link differentiation to any cogent predictions about its relation to apparent technical inefficiency.

Measuring Structural Differentiation

Theoretical analysis suggests that structural differentiation may arise in two sets of circumstances: it may be based on different characteristics embodied in competing brands (where scale economies limit the numbers of combinations of characteristics that can be offered), or it may rest on costs to the buyer of learning about the qualities of the goods offered by rival sellers, with seller-supplied information taking on the function of providing a performance guarantee and also (for goods consumed in public) an "image" that gives utility when consumed jointly with the product. If these models do in fact account for the differentiation evident in industrial markets, how can it be measured with available data? Caves and Williamson (1985) showed that factor analysis of various partial measures of differentiation permits the extraction of factors that behave as if they do indeed measure the structural bases of differentiation.

For this project we extracted principal components from a set of variables that indicate individual dimensions or aspects of differentiation or business decisions made in the light of them. These underlying variables included producers' rates of expenditure on media advertising and also on other forms of sales promotion, the importance of company-financed research and development in the industry (most of which is product oriented and thus related to differentiation), the proportion of output sold to households, an indicator of the unimportance of the product in buyers' total purchases, an indicator that the good is customized for the buyer, an indicator of whether sales promotion is focused on ultimate buyers or on advisers or "specifiers" (for example, physicians in the case of ethical pharmaceuticals), an indicator of the buyer's frequency of purchase, and an indicator of the importance of auxiliary services or assistance provided by seller to buyer.

Interpretations were placed on these components by a process of considering the factor loadings in the light of theoretical guidance about the underlying structural bases for product differentiation. These interpretations are necessarily subjective and should be regarded as maintained hypotheses when we come to examine the statistical relation of the principal components to technical efficiency:

$PC1$ = principal component that indicates positively the unimportance of the product's individual purchases to the buyer ("convenience good") and its affinity for information-based product differentiation; negatively, the component indicates intrinsic complexity and heterogeneity of the product.

$PC2$ = principal component (specifically, second component following $PC1$) that indicates positively the intersection between heterogeneity and information as bases for product differentiation—innovative goods subject to extensive information flows and auxiliary services provided by sellers to buyers.

$PC3$ = principal component (specifically, third component following $PC1$ and $PC2$) that positively indicates that sales-promotion efforts are oriented toward distribution channels or specifiers rather than ultimate buyers.

These three components account for 70 percent of the variance in the underlying variables. We predict no signs of the coefficients of these dimensions of product differentiations because theory indicates only that product differentiation should because expand the variance of the residuals around the production function and not how their skewness might be affected. Only 308 observations are available for these variables; partly for that reason, use was also made of a standard all-purpose indicator of product differentiation.

ADS = inputs of advertising services divided by value of industry shipments.

5.4 Occurrence of Change and Innovation

Hypotheses

Plants' efficiency levels will differ in an industry that is creating or absorbing innovations because the differences among firms in rents or costs will turn up as different revenue/cost relations for their plants. Assume that some firms in an industry offer product innovations and obtain rents insulated from imitation. The resulting lumps of goodwill enlarge the dispersion of plants' apparent efficiency levels, but it is not clear whether measured technical efficiency will increase or decrease. The situation parallels that for trademark-based goodwill assets due to product differentiation.

More tractable for the analysis is the effect of an innovation—product or process—that diffuses through the firms (and thus plants) of an industry. We can think of such an innovation, when first introduced, shifting upward the industry's best-practice frontier and increasing the apparent inefficiency of business units that have not yet adopted it. While new plants or those with worn-out old equipment will adopt it immediately, other units will delay because it does not pay to scrap recent-vintage equipment or "pretty good" products. Diffusion may also be delayed by organizational, cognitive, financial, or competitive factors. Klotz, Madoo, and Hansen (1981) found, as expected, that plants using more modern technology exhibit higher productivity. Shen (1968) found that the productivity advantages of the most efficient plants in an industry are persistent but impermanent. To state his result in terms of our research design, a plant with a positive productivity residual at time t_0 becomes increasingly likely to exhibit a negative residual at t_n, as n increases.[11] In the same vein, the diffusion of any sort of innovation among firms and plants in an industry takes time, and so the greater the incidence of innovation, the wider should be the dispersion of productivity levels below the frontier at any point in time.

An industry's technical efficiency is affected not only by vintage differences in the processes and equipment that it uses but also by the ease with which technical innovations can be incorporated into established plants. Indeed these technical factors can influence apparent efficiency without innovation or technical change—for example, if major unexpected changes in input prices alter the optimal configuration of sunk plant and equipment. The increase in the real price of energy during the early 1970s no doubt expanded the dispersion of plant efficiency levels in some industries. Shen (1970) found that incentives for plants to change their fixed equipment (in his analysis, to grow and to attain scale economies) are mitigated by their past investments in relatively immutable equipment and by institutional difficulties in adopting too many changes too fast (what he called the Penrose effect).

Exogenous Variables

Several variables were employed to measure the decisions or circumstances that would account for elongated tails in industries' efficiency distributions due to the incomplete diffusion of changes. One of these is simply the rate of spending on research and development:

$R&D$ = company-financed research and development spending as a proportion of total sales, 1974–1976.

We expect the apparent extent of technical inefficiency to increase with $R&D$, as Albach (1980) found. In some industries change and productivity growth occur due to innovations made in other industries (such as suppliers of materials or equipment), and their own rates of R&D spending become poor predictors of the rates of internal diffusion of innovations. Therefore, as an alternative to R&D, we employ:

$PROD$ = proportional rate of growth of labor productivity in the industry, 1968–1977.

Like $R&D$, this variable pertains to industries somewhat more aggregated than those in our sample so that its variance is compressed. It should also wield a negative influence on technical efficiency.

Two strategies were used to measure the dispersion of the ages of plants' capital stocks. One draws on the vintage distribution of capital stocks estimated by the Bureau of Labor Statistics, which gives rise to these measures for plant and equipment, respectively:

VINTM = sum of percentage of gross equipment less than five years old and percentage more than twenty years old, 1976.

VINTP = sum of percentage of gross plant less than five years old and percentage more that thirty years old, 1976.

Both measures seek to provide rough indications of the dispersion of the vintages of each industry's capital stock, and apparent technical inefficiency should increase with them.

Another capital-related variable exposes not so much a primary cause of technical inefficiency as a mechanism by which it may arise. The variable is:

SD(K/L) = standard deviation of ratio of adjusted capital stock to adjusted labor input, plants classified to the industry, 1977.

If the production function is homothetic, diverse choices of capital-labor ratios should be associated with several sources of inefficiency. The diversity could result from capital-market imperfections, poor managerial decisions, vintage effects, product diversity, and many other ultimate sources. It could also stem from price or allocative inefficiency—wrong choices of inputs given their prices. Thus if this variable (and others constructed using interplant standard deviations obtained in calculating the frontier production functions) should prove significant, it points to a further inquiry to establish the sources of the diversity.

In 1977 manufacturing industries should have exhibited incompletely diffused adjustments to a major change in input prices. The threefold increase of energy prices in 1973 created a strong incentive for managers in energy-intensive industries to invest in energy-saving equipment or processes. However, planning lags, the 1974–1975 recession, and dispersed vintages of existing equipment meant that the re-equipment process would extend over many years. For most industries it was probably still in full swing in 1977. This adjustment process itself would enlarge the dispersion of apparent efficiency levels, especially in the case of efficiency measured with gross output as the dependent variable. The effect should increase with the importance of energy in an industry's costs, for which we employ:

FUEL = cost of fuels divided by value of industry shipments, 1977.

It should be positively related to technical inefficiency. The data also permit direct observation of the intraindustry dispersions of plants' ratios of fuel to total materials inputs (this information will be used in section 6.3).

5.5 Geographic Market Heterogeneity

Efficiency in an industry can appear to suffer because of several forms of heterogeneity in the geographic markets in which its plants and firms operate. The influence of geographic fragmentation of product markets was noted in section 5.2 in connection with adjusting the measure of seller concentration. However, geographic dispersion should affect apparent technical inefficiency more broadly. A geographically dispersed industry is more likely to face diverse location-specific influences on resource productivity and qualitative differences in inputs.[12] We consider several variables and the influences they might wield on technical efficiency.

The localization of supply in industrial markets can be measured by the distances shipped for manufactured outputs, taken from the Census of Transportation. Two measures were utilized:

DIST = mean distance over which industry tonnage was shipped, 1977.

RAD = radius (miles) within which 80 percent of the industry's tonnage was shipped, 1977.

Low values of *DIST* and *RAD* are consistent with the supplying industry's being fragmented and serving demand in local markets of varying sizes. If geographic fragmentation contributes to apparent technical inefficiency, efficiency should increase with either of these variables.[13]

Another approach to geographic fragmentation hypothesizes that industries processing raw materials will exhibit diverse plant productivity levels due to variations in the quality or location of the raw materials that are processed by individual manufacturing establishments. Whether the resulting differential rents enter into plants' measured productivity levels depends on the distribution of ownership rights. If differential rents turn up on the books of the processors, then technical efficiency should decrease with:

RAW = sum of the industry's input coefficients from primary sectors (agriculture, forestry, fishing, mining).

5.6 Organizational Influences

Our hypotheses hold rather limited relevance to public policy. If the geographic dispersion of an industry or the differentiation of its product increases its apparent technical inefficiency, that is valuable knowledge for extending our understanding of how markets operate, but the conclusion yields few first-order implications for public policy. We now turn to a group of hypotheses that may possess only weak foundations in economic theory but, if supported, hold direct implications for policy. They have to do with the organization of economic activity.

Efficiency of Competing Institutions

The reason that conventional economic theory deals awkwardly with these influences is its Darwinian presumption that the more efficient institution beats out the less efficient one in the marketplace. If a market is served mainly by large, diversified firms that are active in many other industries, the presumption holds that they must enjoy some advantage over specialized firms, individual proprietors, cooperatives, or any other organizational form not legally precluded from undertaking the same activity.

While Darwinian competition is a force to be reckoned with, the speed and directness with which it achieves long-run optimal resource configurations may certainly be questioned. Just as economists recognize sunk costs of specialized plant and equipment, there are sunk costs of achieving coherence in complex organizations, adjusting the expectations of economic agents to the maximum cash flows that they can yield, devising methods of preserving organizations when unanticipated states of nature occur, and so forth. Because of these sunk costs, the Darwinian presumption by no means rules out the prolonged coexistence in a market of competing institutional forms that differ in efficiency.

In this spirit we advance a series of hypotheses about what we might call "institutional splits." Industries are frequently comprised of units that show important institutional differences from one another; among them, single-plant and multiplant firms and unionized and nonunionized establishments. Within our research framework we cannot directly test for differences in the efficiency of the institutional types, but we can test the hypothesis that the dispersion of efficiency levels revealed by our technical-inefficiency measures increases with the prevalence of a suspect institutional type. This test is congenial for hypotheses framed as follows: Institutions A and B are found in an industry, each attaining productivity levels with given means but randomly distributed. B is gradually giving way to A. This pattern could cause the industry's technical inefficiency to increase with the proportion of B institutions if (1) the tail of inefficient B units is longer than the tail of inefficient A units or (2) the mean efficiency of B units is lower, and B no longer holds the dominant share. As these cases suggest, other patterns of Darwinian replacement might fail to reveal themselves in technical inefficiency. A possible example is the displacement of traditional integrated plants by minimills in the U.S. steel industry. With this framework in mind we consider a number of such institutional splits.

Enterprise Diversification

Firms seem less efficient at managing plants located in industries other than those of their basic businesses. Looked at from the viewpoint of the plants classified to a given industry, we might expect those controlled by enterprises classified principally to other industries to be the less efficient. The larger is the proportion of output emanating from plants controlled by outsiders, the greater should be the industry's dispersion of productivity levels.[14] The coverage ratio in the Enterprise Statistics measures this "inbound diversification" to an industry:

$COVE$ = ratio of sales by establishments belonging to enterprises classified to other industries to sales by all establishments classified to this industry.[15]

The hypothesis that the plants controlled by alien enterprises are the less efficient ones predicts a negative effect of $COVE$ on technical efficiency.

Symmetrically firms may be less efficient at managing plants in their basic activities if their top managers are preoccupied with diversification into other industries and thus with the management of resources in diverse economic settings. In that case the more active in other industries are enterprises classified to the industry at hand, the less efficient may be their plants in this industry. This hypothesis calls for a negative effect on efficiency of a variable similar to *COVE*:

SPECE = sales by plants classified to other industries but belonging to firms classified to the industry at hand, divided by sales by all plants belonging to firms classified to this industry.[16]

Major new evidence supporting the hypotheses about *COVE* and *SPECE* has emerged in recent years in findings about the inefficiency of merger-based corporate diversification (Mueller 1985; Ravenscraft and Scherer 1987) and the productivity of management buy outs that restore specialized management (Kaplan 1988).

The hypothesis that diversification may limit productivity can be applied to plants as well as enterprises, as the literature on plant-level diversification shows. The relevant economic model suggests that intraplant diversification trades off the gains from spreading general plant overheads over increased volumes of activity against the diseconomies that arise for coordinating diverse activities under a single plant roof.[17] If plant-level diversification has been overextended, technical efficiency will be negatively related to the complement of the industry's plant-specialization ratio:

SPECP = one minus industry specialization ratio (shipments of products classified to the industry by plants classified to the industry divided by total shipments of those plants).

Klotz, Madoo, and Hansen (1981) found weak evidence of overdiversification.

Multiplant Operation

Many industries contain mixtures of single-plant enterprises and enterprises that operate more than one plant within the industry. Various types of economies of multiplant operation are known to exist (Scherer et al. 1975), but they vary from industry to industry, and there is no intrinsic reason that multiplant operation should always be extended to the optimal degree. On the one hand, efficient multiplant operation might be deterred by the antitrust laws; on the other, the horizontal extension of enterprises for pecuniary gains due to market power could occur despite some cost in technical efficiency. The variable that we use is:

$MULT$ = sales by establishments belonging to companies that are multiplant operators in this industry divided by sales of all establishments classified to the industry.[18]

One special form of multiplant operation needs to be controlled. Companies carry on many nonproduction activities—sales and service, acquisition of inputs, research, general management—that may either be attached to manufacturing establishments or lodged in separate administrative units. In the latter case, the value created by these activities turns up in part in the value of products shipped by the firm's manufacturing establishments, but their costs do not. If all companies active in an industry organized their nonproduction activities in the same way, measured technical efficiency would not be affected by their choice. However, diverse choices are likely; for example, small firms will not have separate administrative establishments, while large companies probably will. We seek to control for this with:

$NPWVAR$ = standard deviation of ratio of nonproduction workers to total employees, plants classified to the industry, multiplied by the industry's overall ratio of nonproduction workers to total employees.

Technical efficiency as measured should decrease with $NPWVAR$. Similar remarks pertain to this variable as to those concerning $SD(K/L)$. Variance in this organizational choice could reflect either optimizing decisions made by differently situated firms or the operation of some force that tends to generate allocative inefficiency. If it takes a significant regression coefficient, further analysis is warranted to establish the underlying causal factors.

Sizes of Production Units

Numerous questions have been raised about the effect of the sizes of enterprises and plants on productivity. These questions address the effectiveness of organizations, in the sense of complex business hierarchies, and the degree of harmony of labor-management relations. Any scale economies in production and nonproduction activities that affect a firm's costs trade off against the intrinsic diseconomies of the organizational hierarchies required to supervise large (in number of employees) enterprises. The diseconomy arises because intrinsic limits on spans of control (the number of supervisees per supervisor) impel the periodic addition of more levels of supervision as the number of primary workers in an activity is increased (Williamson 1967). If this trade-off is not optimized, it can affect the dispersion of plants' efficiency levels. If the problem arises, it is with the larger companies' difficulties of reconciling cost-efficiency with scale-efficiency. Because company-level diversification is already controlled by *COVE* and *SPECE*, we employ the variable:

COSIZE = total industry shipments multiplied by the fraction of industry shipments accounted for by the largest four companies, 1977.

COSIZE indicates the average value of shipments made by the largest four companies classified to the industry.[19]

The potential effect of company size can be addressed in other ways as well. Entrepreneurial effectiveness, and also the predictability of entrepreneurial effectiveness, may vary with company size (and thus typical plant size). Ample empirical evidence indicates that the variance of companies' profit rates, overall or within industries, decreases with their size, supporting the casual observation that small-scale activities attract persons with a high variance of entrepreneurial skills. The managers of larger units, however, must display at least a threshold of competence in order to recruit the services of other factors of production (especially capital). Cutting in the opposite direction is the proposition that complex business organizations (where they are warranted by some form of economies of scale, scope, or network externalities) are difficult to assemble; some combinations may "click," while others do not, and the ways of the more successful ones are not easily imitated by the less successful (Lippman and Rumelt 1982). Thus variations in entrepreneurial effectiveness can cut either way with regard to the effect of companies' (and plants') sizes on the dispersion of efficiency levels.

Because the same arguments can be applied to plants, we also employ a measure of median absolute and relative plant size:

PSIZE = approximate size of the plant accounting for the median unit of industry shipments, measured by value of shipments, 1977.

RSIZE = *PSIZE* divided by value of industry shipments, 1977.

Theory declares no clear preference between these variables. Might large absolute-size plants be more homogeneous in their efficiency because it is worth incurring whatever fixed cost is needed to maintain or restore their efficiency? Are industries with relatively large plants more homogeneous because inefficient (and hence small-share) plants are absent or have been squeezed out? If one embraces the general hypothesis that small plants can exhibit (at least for a time) proportionally lower levels of technical efficiency, *PSIZE* or *RSIZE* should take a positive coefficient, with the better performer depending on the exact mechanism at work.

Labor Relations

A highly controversial question is the effect of labor organization on industrial efficiency. While work rules and craft demarcations can clearly reduce a plant's efficiency (Katz, Kochan, and Keefe 1987), there is also evidence that union organization can increase efficiency by providing a communication channel that resolves grievances and reduces costs associated with employee turnover (Clark 1980; Freeman and Medoff 1984). We employ the variable:

UNION = proportion of production workers who were union
          members, early 1970s.

The state of labor relations may also be related to the variable *PSIZE*, typical plant size. Job satisfaction shows a clear tendency to decline with the size of the employee group in the workplace (Scherer 1976), suggesting that employee-relations problems might increase the variance of productivity levels more in large-plant sectors given the extent of unionization.[20]

Another aspect of labor relations that may affect technical inefficiency is the extent of part-time working in the industry. A fixed cost of setting up an employee in the workplace suggests that part-time labor inputs might give rise to apparent inefficiency (which could be warranted if the reservation wage of part-time workers is lower). On the other hand, a variety of arguments can be made as to why the optimal utilization of part-time employees provides flexibility and adaptability in an activity facing various stochastic elements in its environment. The variable that we employ is:

PART = proportion of part-time workers, estimated from the number
         of hours worked per employee per year (in 1977) on the
         assumption that full-time employees work 2,000 hours a year
         and part-time employees 1,000 hours.

We expect technical efficiency to increase with *PART*. We should keep in mind that part-time working is known to decrease with the size of the employing firm, while *UNION* increases with firm size (Mellow 1982). These two variables are hence likely to be negatively related.

5.7 Omitted Variables

What have we left out? Alas, two interrelated influences of potentially great importance are omitted because we lack means for inferring how they may differ among industries. The first of these is managerial quality or ability. If the managerial task consists of using inputs efficiently and reconfiguring them in the face of changing opportunities, how well this task is performed should be central to the attainment of technical efficiency. Some studies of interfirm differences in technical efficiency have found it associated with the quality or experience of managerial inputs (e.g., Page 1980). And many tests (with or without use of frontier production functions) have found better performance in firms whose managers have stronger incentives to attain efficiency (e.g., Wilson and Jadlow 1982). Managerial shortcomings were found to contribute significantly to differences in the performance of British manufacturing industries relative to their U.S. counterparts (Davies and Caves 1987).

Unfortunately this hypothesis seems incapable of a suitable test by means of interindustry differences. No data are available at the industry level on the quantity and quality of managerial talent they employ. Run-of-the-mill manufacturing industries do not show variations of organizational type that are congenial to exposing differences in the agency situations of their member firms. Interindustry differences in managerial quality, experience, and motivation must therefore go into the error term.

Closely related to this omission is our inability to capture causes of inefficiency in inappropriate record-keeping or decision-making processes used in enterprises. For example, Hayes and Clark (1986) argued that managers miss important opportunities to increase plant efficiency because they work with deceptive and ill-focused cost-accounting data, which (for example) emphasize the saving of direct labor and not information that could expose productivity gains from lower material wastage or rejection rates, less inventory, shorter through-put times, more opportunities for learning and experimentation, and so on. Similarly the business press argues that investment decisions are driven by sources of predictable cash-flow benefit rather than by hard-to-quantify benefits from better quality, adaptation to customers' needs, or ability to adjust to changes.[21] The alleged failures here are not those of competence or incentive but of record-keeping resources and decision-making tools. While these sources of technical inefficiency may or may not deserve the emphasis they currently receive in the ill-focused debate over international competitiveness, they leave no visible tracks in the form of interindustry differences and therefore escape the net of our investigation.

6

Statistical Evidence on Interindustry Determinants

6.1 Issues of Procedure

A number of procedural problems arise in testing the hypotheses about the determinants of technical efficiency. They restrict access to the idealized approach to testing economic models: find the best theoretical model, secure the right data, then perform and report a single test with no "fishing" in the data set. The impediments are:

1. Compared to some other dimensions of market performance, no theoretical model of technical efficiency is strong in its formal underpinning and/or well validated by previous empirical research. At the same time, the manifest significance of technical inefficiency for economic welfare makes the researcher reluctant to miss a robust statistical relationship that might lay claim to a sound but previously unnoticed theoretical basis. How liberally do we experiment with conjectured formulations and interactions that spill beyond the specification proposed in chapter 5?

2. We possess not one measure of technical efficiency but the set whose empirical properties were set forth in chapter 4. These include technical efficiency (EFF), average technical inefficiency (ATI), lambda (λ), and skewness (S), each calculated from production functions with value added (per unit of labor input) and gross output (per employee) as the dependent variables. Should all eight dependent variables be analyzed in parallel, or should the selection be made a priori?

3. Although the total number of industries in the sample is quite large, many of independent variables suffer some missing observations. The holes for different regressors seem largely uncorrelated, so that a model estimated mechancially using the full set of regressors proposed in chapter 5 will utilize only about one-fourth of the observations on the dependent variable. Similarly shifts in specifica-

tion of the model sometimes induce substantial changes in the number of observations available. Do we ignore this problem, or do we approach the estimation piecewise, paying attention to which variables cost the most degrees of freedom?

4. Cross-section research designs in industrial organization usually encounter multicollinearity, and the regressors in this model overlap sufficiently with those used in previous studies to ensure its presence. Do we ignore that threat, or do we address it indirectly (the only direct fix is "better data") by emphasizing the degree to which rejections of the null hypothesis are robust with respect to changes in the model's specification?

5. Heteroskedasticity is expected because the dependent variables are derived from coefficients that are estimated with levels of precision that differ from industry to industry (Saxonhouse 1976). What approach should be employed for dealing with that problem, and at what stage in the research should it be introduced?

Because these considerations interact with each other, we addressed them as a group. In the light of the first and third problems, a significant amount of experimentation was indulged, putting up front the exogenous variables with the strongest rationales and the fewest missing values, leaving theoretically weaker variables and those with many missing observations for later consideration. Parallel to this, we based our acceptance or rejection of individual hypotheses in part on the robustness of their performance in response to changes in specification and in the available number of degrees of freedom. This somewhat inductive approach did not, however, include experimenting with alternative dependent variables; the theoretical and empirical case for technical efficiency estimated from production functions employing value added per unit of labor input led us to perform the analysis with that dependent variable alone. After determining the hypotheses that were accepted and rejected with that dependent variable, we fitted the same model to the alternative dependent variables and observed the effect on the results. Finally, the sequential procedures described were carried out prior to applying a correction for heteroskedasticity; this correction was applied to models that had been found to give the most defensible representation of the OLS results.

The chosen treatment of heteroskedasticity needs to be explained at the outset. We expected the problem of heteroskedasticity due to the differences among industries in the variance of the estimated coefficients that underlie the dependent variable. Heteroskedasticity with respect to regressors was also likely. We approached the former problem indirectly. Although a standard error of the measure of technical efficiency can in principle be calculated, it appeared more sensible to proceed indirectly by using the standard error of estimate of the underlying production function as our indicator of the variance of the technical-efficiency measure.[1] Using Gorringe's procedures (suggested by Johnston 1972, pp. 220–221), we regressed absolute values of the residuals from the core regression model on that variable and on the regressors in the model. Surprisingly we found no evidence of the "Saxonhouse problem." Furthermore, among the regressors, heteroskedasticity appeared to be concentrated in a single variable although powerfully present for that variable. With heteroskedasticity apparently confined this way to the regressors, we simply used White's (1980) procedure to secure consistent standard errors, which are reported in all models that follow.[2]

The preferred dependent variable, technical efficiency (EFF), is theoretically bounded between 0 and 1, as is the alternative ATI. These variables were entered in log-odds form into the estimations reported below.

6.2 Main Statistical Findings

It is convenient to start with a model that presents those results that have proved robust and possesses a comfortably large number of degrees of freedom:

$$EFF = \begin{array}{cccc} 1.054^{aa} & - 0.116^a \; NOBS & - 0.013^a \; VINTM & - 0.013^a \; SD(K/L) \\ (12.08) & (29.32) & (6.73) & (12.48) \end{array}$$

$$\begin{array}{cccc} - 0.044^{aa} \; R\&D & - 0.463^a \; DIV & + 3.964^a \; RSIZE & + 0.837^{aa} \; PART \\ (2.77) & (8.90) & (17.81) & (3.35) \end{array}$$

$$\bar{R}^2 = 0.525 \quad \text{d.f.} = 277$$

The notation that we shall employ throughout this chapter for significance levels is $a = 1$ percent, $b = 5$ percent, and $c = 10$ percent in one-tail tests; when two-tail tests are deemed appropriate, we double the superscripts to indicate corresponding two-tail significance levels. The variable NOBS is the square root of the number of observations, derived in section 4.3 as the appropriate correction for the link between the efficiency measure and number of establishments observed in calculating the frontier production functions, on the basis of order statistics. Its coefficient is highly significant, and its potent influence tells us that any findings about the effect of competitive conditions (also dependent on the number of participants in the market) will be highly sensitive to acceptance of the interpretation of *NOBS* as a correction for an order-statistics effect.

The regression coefficients have no direct interpretation; they are not elasticities. For variables with important implications for economic behavior and/or policy, we calculated an effect in terms of how many standard deviations in the overall distribution an industry's technical efficiency would be raised by a stated change in an exogenous variable. Because the estimation was done with the dependent variable in log-odds form, an improvement of one standard deviation cannot be translated directly into a percentage improvement in technical efficiency; however, as a rough indication, one standard deviation of *EFF* in natural units is 17 percent. Raising *RSIZE* by one standard deviation (8.9 percent of the market) would have a large effect, raising technical efficiency by about 0.3 standard deviation. Raising the part-time worker proportion (*PART*) by one standard deviation (also about 8.9 percent) would increase efficiency by only 0.05 standard deviation. An industry that does no research and development rather than the mean level would report its technical efficiency to be elevated by about 0.04 standard deviation, while an industry with its equipment-vintage distribution (*VINTM*) lowered by one standard deviation rather than the mean level would report about 0.08 standard deviation more efficiency. Most important for policy, lowering enterprise diversification (an average mix of inbound and outbound) by 10 percentage points would raise efficiency by 0.04 standard deviation (lowering diversification by one standard deviation would raise it by 0.1 standard deviation).

Now consider the groups of hypotheses from chapter 5. The preceding equation contains no variables that primarily represent competitive conditions; competitive conditions can be measured in diverse ways. Also missing is any variable bearing on the heterogeneity and differentiation of the product; as was noted in chapter 5, differentiation could decrease measured technical efficiency, or it could merely increase the dispersion of plants' productivity levels symmetrically around their mean. Nonetheless, some positive findings will be set out below. Geographic heterogeneity exerted no robust influence and is absent from the core model. Two variables represent heterogeneity due to inputs and technology choices. The dispersion of the vintages of an industry's equipment (but not its plant), *VINTM*, significantly decreases measured technical efficiency. We thus confirm Shen's (1968) finding that capital-vintage effects are important for observed technical efficiency (also Førsund and Hjalmarsson 1987). The other significant factor relating to capital is the dispersion of capital-labor ratios for the industry's plants (*SD(K/L)*). Because this variable begs the question of what more fundamental structural or behavioral forces might cause the dispersion of plants' *K/L* ratios, we examine its determinants in section 6.3.

The three remaining variables relate to the organization of inputs and production in the industry. The first of these is *DIV*, the sum of the measures of inbound (*COVE*) and outbound (*SPECE*) diversification introduced in chapter 5. This variable indicates that at the 1 percent confidence level, technical efficiency decreases with the extent of enterprise-level diversification into and out of the industry. This finding contributes importantly, we feel, to the debate over corporate mergers. Its statistical underpinning will be considered further.

A second organization variable is the size of an efficient-scale plant relative to the market, *RSIZE*, which positively affects technical efficiency. The prevalence of large-share plants seems to be associated with the squeeze-out or absence of small-share units with more variable efficiency levels. A third organizational factor is the extent to which part-time employees are utilized in an industry; its positive influence suggests that flexibility pays off in the efficienct use of resources. *PART* is collinear with the extent of union membership, a variable whose influence is discussed below.

Other results we report were obtained jointly with or conditional on all or most of the results reported in the preceding equation. We now take the groups of hypotheses and report more fully on the fates of the individual variables.

Competitive Conditions and International Trade

As an additive variable in linear form, the concentration of domestic producers has no influence on technical efficiency. This is shown in table 6.1, equation 1.[3] That negative finding is not surprising in the light of the discussion in chapter 5. We did find an influence, not always coherent or robust to specification changes, when concentra-

Table 6.1
Results on interindustry determinants of technical efficiency related to competitive conditions

Equation number	Equation	$\bar{R}^2$/d.f.
1.	-0.013^a VINTM $- 0.464^a$ DIV $+ 0.0003$ CONC	0.524
	(6.73)　　　　　　(8.92)　　　　　(0.21)	277
2.	-0.185^a VIOL▸C2 $+ 0.048^{bb}$ VIOL∗C3 $- 0.062$ VIOL∗C4	0.490
	(3.43)　　　　　　　(2.21)　　　　　　　(0.65)	317
3.	-0.014^a VINTM $- 0.299^a$ DIV $+ 0.531^{aa}$ C4AJ $- 0.655^{bb}$ C4AJ^2	0.563
	(8.43)　　　　　　(6.86)　　　　　(2.77)　　　　　(2.39)	233
4.	-0.015^a VINTM $- 0.275^a$ DIV $+ 0.005^c$ MS	0.542
	(9.29)　　　　　　(7.30)　　　　　(1.66)	163
5.	-0.014^a VINTM $- 0.263^a$ DIV $+ 0.0002^a$ MS∗XC	0.543
	(9.01)　　　　　　(6.99)　　　　　(10.59)	163
6.	-0.017^a VINTM $- 0.225^a$ DIV $+ 0.006^b$ MS $- 0.007^{aa}$ XS	0.566
	(10.64)　　　　　　(6.63)　　　　　(1.95)　　　　　(4.14)	153

Note: Each equation also includes a constant term and the variables NOBS, SD(K/L), R&D, RSIZE, and PART. Where one-tail tests of significance are appropriate, a = 1 percent, b = 5 percent, and c = 10 percent; where two-tail tests of significance are appropriate, aa = 1 percent, bb = 5 percent, and cc = 10 percent.

tion is interacted with other variables. The first of these is VIOL, the incidence of antitrust indictments. We divided the sampled industries into quartiles, omitting the least concentrated quartile and defining C2, C3 and C4 as dummies indicating that an industry falls, respectively, in the second, third, or highest quartile. When each dummy is multiplied by VIOL, we get the result reported in table 6.1, equation 2. A highly significant negative effect of collusion appears in moderately concentrated industries—the second quartile, with four-firm concentration ranging from 0.32 to 0.45. By itself this result seems consistent with most estimates of the threshold at which collusive activities start to become feasible (for example, Bradburd and Over 1982). However, previous empirical evidence implies that the negative effect should continue into the third quartile, yet the coefficient of VIOL∗C3 is positive and indeed significant at 5 percent in a two-tail test.[4] For the most concentrated industries, where collusion might be expected to have little or no effect on technical efficiency, the coefficient is again negative but insignificant. The pattern of inconsistent evidence, along with the shaky foundations of the hypothesis itself, [5] causes us to accept the null hypothesis.

A large empirical literature lends support to the concentration ratio itself as an effective summary statistic for competitive conditions in an industry.[6] In general the degree of rivalry in industrial markets decreases with the concentration ratio, but there are important reasons that the decreasing relation may not be linear. We therefore entered the concentration ratio as adjusted by Weiss and Pascoe (for international competition, regional fragmentation, and misdefinition of the market) in a quadratic form. As equation 3 shows, both the adjusted concentration ratio and its square take significant coefficients, which imply a maximum level of efficiency at an adjusted concentration ratio of 40.5 percent. That is just above the sample mean (38.9 percent) and below the threshold range (45 to 55 in most studies) in which appreciable deviations from a purely competitive outcome begin to surface. The number-of-observations effect inhibits drawing any strong conclusions, but the data are consistent with the hypothesis that efficiency declines with the industry's scope for departures from pure competition.

Import competition was also investigated directly, along with the industry's participation in exports. On the basis of theoretical considerations (not to mention the casual evidence highly visible in the past decade), we would have assigned international competition a premier role among the forces expected to affect technical efficiency, despite the decline by one-fifth of the U.S. dollar's trade-weighted real value between 1971 and 1977. However, the affliction of missing data forced this variable's omission from the core model.[7] When imports' share of domestic supply (MS) is added as a linear term, it takes the expected positive sign but its t-value falls short of 5 percent significance (see equation 4). When it is interacted with the conventional concentration ratio, that result stays unchanged. In equation 5 it is interacted with a different measure of concentration suggested by the significant positive influence on efficiency of $RSIZE$. That is XC, which is the four-firm concentration ratio minus the minimum level of concentration that would be observed if the largest four firms each operated a single plant of estimated minimum efficient scale—"excess concentration" over that warranted by plant-scale economies. The coefficient of $MS*XC$ is positive and significant at the 1 percent level. Participation in exporting activities (XS) is negatively related to technical efficiency (see equation 6). It supports the hypothesis that any procompetitive

effect of exporting activity may be swamped by the uneven distribution of quasi-rents and apparent technical inefficiency that exporting
is likely to produce.[8] Increasing import competition by one standard
deviation (an increase of 10 percentage points in imports/new supply)
raises an industry's efficiency by 0.05 standard deviation. In short,
import competition has become a strong factor enforcing technical
efficiency on U.S. manufacturing industries with high concentration
levels that are not due to production-scale economies. Exporting activities decrease apparent technical efficiency in the same way as R&D
outlays: the resource-productivity benefits that export opportunities
generate are spread unevenly among firms and plants, making the
nonparticipants look inefficient.

Product Differentiation and Other Heterogeneity

We now consider detailed results on the effect of product differentiation and other natural sources of heterogeneity in plants' productivity
levels. Product differentiation should increase the dispersion of producers' revenue-productivity, because the appeal of characteristics of
different brands or the efficacy of their promotion may vary persis-
tently. This increased dispersion may but need not translate into increased technical inefficiency. The variables developed in chapter 5 to
measure differentiation seek to transcend the traditional proxy—the
advertising-sales ratio—with a more complex measure based on principal components that captures something of the basis for differentiation in the product's structural complexity and the lock-ins that it
creates between supplier and customer.

In table 6.2 equation 1 includes the customary measure of product
differentiation, the advertising–sales ratio (ADS). Its coefficient is
negative—consistent with generating apparent inefficiency—and
statistically significant.[9] Equation 2 illustrates our alternative approach of employing principal components to control for the complex nature of product differentiation. The significant coefficient of
PC1, the first principal component, indicates that apparent technical
efficiency is reduced by the presence of differentiation by advertising
of products that represent unimportant purchases to the buyer, while
it is increased or at least not impaired by the structural complexity
of the product. Industries producing consumer convenience goods
typically contain cores of firms producing strongly differentiated and
successful brands, surrounded by fringes of less differentiated pro-

Table 6.2
Results on interindustry determinants of technical efficiency related to structural heterogeneity

Equation number	Equation	$\bar{R}^2$/d.f.
1.	$-0.012^a\ VINTM - 0.459^a\ DIV - 1.965^a\ ADS$ (6.71) (9.80) (2.36)	0.511 251
2.	$-0.008^a\ VINTM - 0.412^a\ DIV - 0.066^{aa}\ PC1 + 0.033\ PC2$ (5.45) (10.02) (4.60) (0.13)	0.491 193
3.	$-0.014^a\ VINTM - 0.091^a\ DIV + 0.00008^a\ RAD$ (8.92) (2.50) (2.60)	0.527 193
4.	$-0.012^a\ VINTM - 0.445^a\ DIV - 0.181\ RAW$ (6.10) (8.57) (0.93)	0.526 270
5.	$-0.014^a\ VINTM - 0.500^a\ DIV + 0.060\ PROD$ (7.07) (9.87) (0.72)	0.520 277
6.	$-0.013^a\ VINTM - 0.444^a\ DIV + 1.911^{cc}\ FUEL$ (6.48) (8.51) (1.73)	0.526 276

Note: See note to table 6.1.

ducers with little market power; apparently the rents accruing to the former influence the estimated position of the industry's efficiency frontier. Insignificant were successive principal components PC2 and PC3 (not shown) indicating, respectively, an interaction of product heterogeneity and information as bases for differentiation and promotion oriented to advisers or specifiers.

Another source of structural heterogeneity in plants' productivity levels is localization due to transport costs, measured inversely by the variable RAD, the radius within which 80 percent of U.S. producers' shipments move outbound from the plant. In equation 3 its positive and significant coefficient indicates that more localized industries exhibit more apparent inefficiency.[10] Replaced by its alternative DIST, the coefficient becomes less significant. We also tested whether input heterogeneity, reflected by the importance of primary inputs (RAW), reduces measured technical efficiency. In equation 4 the coefficient of RAW is negative but not significant.

Innovation and Change

The core regression model showed that measured technical efficiency decreases with the importance of an industry's spending on research and development. That result might hold either because the rents imputed to plants belonging to innovative firms make plants not attached to research-oriented firms appear inefficient or because incompletely diffused innovations amplify the differences among plants' revenue-productivity levels. We can shed a little light on those competing interpretations by replacing R&D with another measure, the industry's rate of productivity growth (PROD). The sign of its coefficient is inappropriately positive (but insignificant) in equation 5 of table 6.2. Therefore the appearance of technical inefficiency seems more likely to arise because of high productivity levels for the industry's innovative leaders than from the incomplete diffusion of innovations.

We already reported that vintage effects (VINTM) and diverse choices of technology (SD(K/L)) contribute significantly to technical inefficiency. The dispersion of the distribution of ages of plant (VINTP) fails to exert a significant effect parallel to that of VINTM; however, one might expect productivity to be less closely tied to the age of plant than to the age of machinery in most industries.

With the analysis based on 1977, four years after the first energy shock (1973), we expected to find measured technical inefficiency affected by the incomplete adoption of new energy-saving technologies for industries in which energy's cost is important; however, the data revealed no evidence whatever of this effect. Both the importance of fuel costs to the industry (FUEL) and the dispersion of plants' fuel cost/materials inputs ratios in an industry take wrong-signed (positive) coefficients (see equation 6). The dispersion of capital–labor ratios (SD(K/L)), a significant negative influence in the core model, may be partly due to incomplete fuel economization; in section 6.3 that question is considered in a general investigation of the forces lying behind the measures of interplant variances.

Organizational Influences

Organizational influences are particularly important among the regressors because of their implications for business decisions and public policy. Evidence was already reported that corporate diversification, plant scales, and some aspects of employment contracts (part-time work) affect technical efficiency.

Because of the importance of our finding on diversification, we sought assurance that it was not due to collinearity with other vari-

Table 6.3
Results on interindustry determinants of technical efficiency related to economic organization

Equation number	Equation	$\bar{R}^2$/d.f.
1.	-0.544^b $COVE(HR\&D) - 0.674^a$ $COVE(LR\&D)$ (3.39) (5.53) -0.327^c $SPECE$ (2.43)	0.511 279
2.	-0.013^a $VINTM - 0.411^a$ $DIV - 0.004$ $UNION$ (6.87) (8.01) (1.54)	0.527 256
3.	-0.0008 $UNION(SP) - 0.005^a$ $UNION(LP) - 0.246^{bb}$ LPD (0.59) (3.32) (2.11)	0.507 259
4.	-0.639^a $COVE(HR\&D) - 0.619^a$ $COVE(LR\&D)$ (4.26) (5.41) -2.719^a $NPWVAR - 0.010^a$ $UNION*LPS$ (3.10) (3.83)	0.516 258
5.	-0.013^a $VINTM - 0.435^a$ $DIV - 0.00006^{bb}$ $COSIZE$ (6.67) (9.09) (2.42)	0.524 276

Note: See note to table 6.1.

ables. A prime suspect was research and development activities because of their importance in industries that display high levels of diversification, with diversification serving to raise the utilization of any proprietary knowledge relevant to more than a single product or industry (Lemelin 1982; MacDonald 1985). In addition, R&D activity was found to exert a significant negative influence on measured technical efficiency . To make sure that *DIV*'s influence was not due to its association with *R&D*, we allowed the variables *COVE* and *SPECE* to take different coefficients depending on whether *R&D* was greater or less than its mean in the sample. Equation 1 of table 6.3 shows that the negative influence on technical efficiency of inbound diversification (*COVE*) is somewhat larger and more significant in the low-R&D (*LR&D*) than the high-R&D (*HR&D*) industries.[11] Thus the negative effect of inbound diversification is, if anything, more pronounced where research and innovation are unimportant, though not only there. No corresponding difference is found for outbound diversification (*SPECE*), which appears uninteracted in equation 1.[12] We also observe that outbound diversification exerts a smaller and less significant depressing effect than inbound diversification. The sensible implication is that companies can manage plants carrying on their principal activities better than they can manage plants in other industries, although their base activities do suffer some from managerial attention diverted to diversified holdings.

We now turn to the labor-organization variables. Recent empirical research has indicated that union membership need not be unfavorable for productivity overall. However, problems associated with work rules and seniority protection seem more likely to make it a negative factor in industries where technology compels large plant sizes. The proportion of an industry's work force whose employees are union members (UNION) has a negative but insignificant influence on technical efficiency. It t-value is -1.54 in equation 2 of table 6.3, less significant in most other additive specifications. To test for a differential effect in large-plant industries, we calculated for each industry the average absolute size of the larger plants that account for one-half of its output and then used its mean to separate industries into those with greater (LP) and smaller (SP) sizes of their larger plants. In equation 3 UNION is allowed to take a different coefficient in each sector; we also include LPD as an intercept-shift dummy for large-plant industries. The results point to a significant negative effect of union membership in large-plant industries.[13] Increasing an industry's union membership by one standard deviation (12.4 percentage points) lowers its efficiency by 0.038 standard deviation (equation 2) or by 0.047 standard deviation in large-plant industries (equation 3).

In equation 4 we present an alternative form of this interaction, multiplying UNION by the mean size of the industry's large plants (LPS). This interaction's negative coefficient is significant at 1 percent; however, it retreats to 10 percent in the absence of the variable NPWVAR, the weighted standard deviation of ratios of nonproduction workers to total employees for plants classified to the industry. This variable, like $SD(K/L)$, depicts a form of heterogeneity in an industry's plants that could well increase measured technical inefficiency, but it does not explain why the heterogeneity occurs (see section 6.3). NPWVAR's coefficient is always negative, and it is significant in most specifications.

Union membership is collinear with other variables that address the industry's labor organization. It is negatively correlated with part-time employment (PART) and tends to reduce but not eliminate the significance of that variable's coefficient. UNION is positively correlated with the average wage of production workers; if that variable is added to the model, it takes a positive and marginally significant coefficient. The coefficients and significance levels of these variables are naturally sensitive to the inclusion or exclusion of others. Our data base does not permit a sharp discrimination among the influences that these variables wield on technical efficiency except to establish that the positive effect of *PART* and the negative effect of unionization in large-plant industries are significant but not precisely estimated. The flexibility of part-time employment increases technical efficiency, but that effect may be in part due to or accompanied by a tendency for high-wage industries to show high technical efficiency and/or efficiency to be impaired by unionization in large-plant industries.

The other hypotheses about business organization addressed absolute sizes of companies and the extent of multiplant operation. Neither multiplant operation within an industry nor the absolute sizes of plants (apart from the interaction with unionization) exhibit any influence on technical efficiency. However, in equation 5 the average absolute size (measured by base-industry sales) of the four largest companies (*COSIZE*) exerts a negative effect. It is significant at the 5 percent level of confidence (two-tail test), but its significance depends on making the correction for heteroskedasticity. Notice that a company's size within an industry is at least potentially independent of diversification, and the presence of *COSIZE* in the model reduces neither the magnitude nor the significance of *DIV*'s coefficient. On the other hand, the negative role of the number of competitiors (*NOBS*), the positive effect of relative plant size (*RSIZE*), and the negative effect of diversification (*DIV*) represent influences sufficiently related to *COSIZE* that we are disinclined to push this conclusion with great confidence.[14]

6.3 What Lies behind Intraindustry Variances?

From the calculation of the stochastic frontier productions on the first phase of this project we obtained as by-products a number of novel statistics concerning the heterogeneity of the activities of those plants classified to an industry and entering into our sample (the Annual Survey of Manufactures panel). They take the forms of standard deviations and coefficients of variation calculated (unweighted) from the data on the reporting plants. Three were tested as determinants of technical efficiency, and two of them proved statistically significant: (*SD(K/L)*, the standard deviation of capital-labor ratios, and

NPWVAR, the standard deviation of the ratio of nonproduction workers to total employed weighted by its industry means.

To blame inefficiency on these variances is unsatisfying, as we noted. Other structural determinants correspond either to explicit behavioral sources of persistent inefficiency or to structural sources of heterogeneity that are external to managers' decisions about the use of resources. Heterogeneities that directly reflect those decisions merely transfer attention to the exogenous factors that cause or permit managers to make these heterogeneous allocations. A major investigation could be built around that question alone. Although the analysis that follows is only exploratory, the dependent variables are both novel and appropriate for testing most of the obvious hypotheses.

Descriptive Patterns

Because these data may hold interest for other investigators, we provide some descriptive statistics before turning to the causal analysis. Table 6.4 lists the measures of input heterogeneity obtained for each industry from the computation of the frontier production functions. For each variable and industry we calculated the unweighted mean value and standard deviation over all the plants included in the Annual Survey panel. These are designated as intraindustry standard deviations and means. Table 6.4 presents summary statistics calculated across 436 industries.[15] Column 1 contains the mean calculated across industries of the intraindustry standard deviations. We also calculated the average across industries of the intraindustry means and in column 2 divided this into the interindustry mean standard deviation. Column 2 can be thought of roughly as a coefficient of variation that shows the measure's variability among plants in the typical industry. Column 3 reports the coefficient of variation calculated across the 436 industries of the standard deviations used to obtain the mean reported in column 1. That is, column 3 roughly indicates how much the interplant dispersions vary among the 436 industries.

We now consider the specific dimensions of plants' input structures and activities. The first line of table 6.4 refers to the capital-labor ratio, where capital includes the imputed value of rented plant and equipment, and labor measures the plant work force in terms of effective production worker hours (the difference between production and nonproduction worker compensation is used to convert nonproduc-

Table 6.4
Descriptive statistics: Measures of heterogeneity of establishments classified
to four-digit SIC industries

Variable (standard deviation)	Mean standard deviation (1)	Mean standard deviation/mean of means (2)	Coefficient of variation (3)
Adjusted capital/adjusted labor	116.95	0.99	1.195
Machinery/total capital	0.15	0.38	0.205
Fuel + electricity/materials inputs	0.06	0.95	0.869
Capital expenditures/capital stock	10.81	1.58	0.446
Nonproduction workers/ employees	0.12	0.16	0.323
Production worker hourly wage	1.47	0.27	0.351
Value added/adjusted labor hours	10.70	0.70	1.298

Note: Observations were taken on 435 or 436 industries for each variable.
Stated more fully, the column definitions are (1) unweighted average over 436
industries of the standard deviation of the stated variable calculated across
plants classified to each industry; (2) ratio of (1) to mean calculated over 436
industries of the (unweighted) mean of the stated variable calculated over
each industry's plants; (3) coefficient of variation of (1), i.e., a measure of the
dispersion of the standard deviations of the stated variable over 436 industries.

tion labor into production labor equivalents). The variable designated
as capital expenditures/capital stock is based on each plant's capital
expenditures in 1977 relative to its capital stock in that year; the interplant variance of this measure should indicate the lumpiness or dis-
continuity of capital expenditures by ongoing plants in the industry.
The definitions of other variables listed in table 6.4 are obvious from
their names.

The table yields several impressionistic conclusions. Capital-labor
ratios are strikingly variable within the typical industry, and their dispersion differs greatly by industry. The intensity of fuel use also is
both highly variable in the typical industry and differs in its variability
from industry to industry (despite its failure to surface as a determinant of technical efficiency). Given the abundant evidence that capital
and energy are complementary in production, one wonders if the
conclusions about the interplant variability of these inputs are also

related. By contrast, the nonproduction worker components of plants' work forces do not vary much in the typical industry, nor are their patterns particularly dissimilar from one industry to the next. While production worker wages show appreciable variability in the typical industry, the ratio of value added to labor is much more variable—a pattern that has been noticed in other studies and one that prevails both among plants and among industries.

Causes of Interplant Differences: Capital/Labor

Chapter 2 supplied the conceptual groundwork specifying variables associated with differences in plants' input structures. The theory of efficiency measurement distinguishes between technical and allocative or price inefficiency. The key dependent variable in our own study is a technical-efficiency measure that might or might not be correlated with allocative efficiency. The diversity variables listed in table 6.4 are direct measures of allocative differences among plants. They reflect some combination of outright allocative inefficiency (nonoptimal input choices), diverse efficient choices due to heterogeneous prices or supply conditions in input markets, nonhomotheticity in production functions, and random factors. The hypothetical determinants of these diversity measures should therefore include indicators of diversity (distortions?) in factor supplies, as well as any structural variables that might foster or abet allocative inefficiency.

The first and most important dependent variable is $SD(K/L)$, the interplant (intraindustry) standard deviation of the capital-labor ratio. Because both K and L are positive, we expect the variable to increase with the industry's (unweighted) mean capital-labor ratio ($MEAN (K/L)$), and equations 1 and 2 of table 6.5 show that this is powerfully the case. If differences in local labor-market conditions impose diverse wage costs on plants, we would expect $SD(K/L)$ to increase with the interplant standard deviation of wages per production worker ($SD(WAGE)$), and this coefficient is also positive and significant at 5 percent (one-tail test). We found that part-time workers apparently serve as a source of flexibility and thus efficiency. The effective use of part-time workers presumably affects the configuration of capital, as well as allowing a larger number of labor-hours to be utilized along with a given capital stock. In equation 1 we accordingly find that $SD(K/L)$ increases significantly with $PART$.

Table 6.5
Regression models of determinants of interplant (intraindustry) dispersions
of input structure

Number	Regression equation

1. $SD(K/L) = -10.70 + 0.752 \, MEAN(K/L) + 2.031 \, SD(WAGE)$
     $\quad\quad\quad\quad (8.78)\quad(19.4)\quad\quad\quad\quad\quad (1.86)$

     $\quad + 1.439 \, PROD + 9.389 \, PART + 33.72 \, SD(MACH/K)$
     $\quad\quad (2.01)\quad\quad\quad\quad (2.43)\quad\quad\quad (3.46)$
     $\quad\quad\quad\quad\quad\quad\quad\quad\quad\quad\quad\quad\quad \bar{R}^2 = 0.882; \text{ d.f.} = 428$

2. $SD(K/L) = -4.94 + 0.747 \, MEAN(K/L) + 2.165 \, SD(WAGE)$
     $\quad\quad\quad\quad (4.94)\quad(20.9)\quad\quad\quad\quad\quad (2.10)$

     $\quad + 1.776 \, PROD - 0.018 \, VINTM + 0.002 \, SPECP$
     $\quad\quad (2.41)\quad\quad\quad\quad (0.95)\quad\quad\quad\quad (0.22)$

     $\quad + 0.050 \, SD(DK/K)\quad\quad\quad\quad \bar{R}^2 = 0.888; \text{ d.f.} = 412$
     $\quad\quad (0.51)$

3. $FUELVAR = 0.013 + 0.0004 \, MEAN(K/L) + 0.0001 \, VINTP$
     $\quad\quad\quad\quad\quad (4.35)\quad (2.87)\quad\quad\quad\quad\quad\quad (0.97)$

     $\quad - 0.0004 \, VINTM\quad\quad\quad\quad \bar{R}^2 = 0.140; \text{ d.f.} = 425$
     $\quad\quad (4.12)$

4. $NPWVAR = 0.081 + 0.140 \, ADS + 3.150 \, R\&D + 0.003 \, RAW$
     $\quad\quad\quad\quad\quad (57.3)\quad (3.24)\quad\quad\quad (5.16)\quad\quad\quad (0.43)$

     $\quad + 0.003 \, COVE + 0.0002 \, XS\quad\quad \bar{R}^2 = 0.078; \text{ d.f.} = 286$
     $\quad\quad (0.85)\quad\quad\quad\quad (2.27)$

5. $NPWVAR = 0.089 + 2.057 \, R\&D + 0.015 \, RAW + 0.006 \, PC1$
     $\quad\quad\quad\quad\quad (7.60)\quad (2.64)\quad\quad\quad (2.42)\quad\quad\quad (6.73)$

     $\quad + 0.007 \, PC2\quad\quad\quad\quad\quad \bar{R}^2 = 0.188; \text{ d.f.} = 297$
     $\quad\quad (6.04)$

We considered whether $SD(K/L)$ is closely related to any available
measures of the heterogeneity of establishments' capital stocks. That
heterogeneity would be greater where technical progress is rapid and/
or the vintage distribution of machinery and plant is more dispersed.
In equations 1 and 2 the coefficients of $PROD$, the growth rate of the
industry's labor productivity over 1968–1977, is appropriately positive and significant. However, the coefficients of $VINTM$ (equation 2)
and $VINTP$ (not shown) are insignificant. Is the heterogeneity of an
industry's K/L values associated with the mix of plant and equipment? In equation 1 the coefficient of the interplant (intraindustry)
standard deviation of the ratio of machinery to total capital

($SD(MACH/K)$) is positive and highly significant. Is the heterogeneity due to differences in the output diversification of plants classified to the industry? In equation 2 this hypothesis is rejected by an insignificant coefficient for $SPECP$, the complement of the industry's plant specialization ratio. Finally we wondered whether the heterogeneity of K/L is due to the lumpiness of new investment, measured by $SD(DK/K)$, the interplant (intraindustry) standard deviation of ratios of capital expenditure in 1977 to capital stock. In equation 2 its coefficient is positive but not significant.

Do these findings about $SD(K/L)$ modify or extend our general conclusions about the determinants of technical efficiency? The variance of that regressor clearly does reflect the diversity of plant-level choices of both capital and labor inputs. In that sense it serves as a summary statistic for several diversities of input choices. While the results contained in table 6.5 hardly support any unqualified policy conclusions, we can usefully draw out its implications by noting the polices that might lie behind the results. The dispersion of K/L increases with the diversity of wages; if the wage dispersion results from union rent seeking (rather than differentials that properly reflect opportunity costs), a real social cost would be involved. The prevalence of part-time workers, already revealed as a source of efficiency in our basic model of technical efficiency, is shown to exert at least some of its influence through interplant differences in capital stocks. While this linkage reduces $PART$'s net positive contribution to technical efficiency, it also suggests that managerial practices that eschew the use of part-time workers are probably inefficient. Finally, and more obviously, the choices that managers make about renewing their machinery stocks seem to exert substantial leverage on technical efficiency, underlining the importance of appropriately designed public policies toward taxation and investment incentives.

Causes of Interplant Differences: Energy Use

Contrary to our expectations, fuel-intensive industries did not appear technically inefficient in 1977 as a result of incomplete adapations to the 1973 energy-price shock. In equation 3 the intraindustry variance of plants' ratios of fuel to total purchased materials ($FUELVAR$) is regressed on several variables. It turns out to be closely related to industries' mean capital–labor ratios ($MEAN(K/L)$), illustrating the complementarity of energy and capital as inputs and implying that some effect on technical efficiency of incomplete adjustments to high energy prices is captured by coefficient of $SD(K/L)$. We also include in equation 3 the dispersions of the vintages of both plant and equipment; the coefficient of $VINTP$ is positive as expected but not significant, and that of $VINTM$ is inexplicably negative and significant.

Causes of Interplant Differences: Nonproduction Workers

The interplant weighted standard deviation of nonproduction workers' share of employment ($NPWVAR$) should increase with the importance of specific types of nonproduction activities to an industry. In equations 4 and 5 $R\&D$ proves to be a significant source of this variance. In equation 4 the advertising-sales ratio (ADS) is also significant, but its coefficient is much smaller than that of $R\&D$ (their units are comparable). In equation 5 ADS is replaced by the principal components measuring product differentiation. The coefficient of $PC1$ is highly significant and indicates large interplant differences in nonproduction activities for products that are in widespread use but individually unimportant purchases subject to heavy advertising (for example, many consumer nondurables). The highly significant positive coefficient of $PC2$ reflects its designation of products for which sales forces transmit large amounts of information to buyers. These results make sense in that most advertising services are purchased outside the firm (plant), while research and distribution activities are commonly integrated. The importance of raw material inputs (RAW) and the prevalence of inbound diversification ($COVE$) have no significant influence. Previous research (Caves 1986) suggests that the uneven participation of firms and establishments in exporting activities could be a source of dispersion; accordingly in equation 4 the coefficient of XS is positive and significant.

6.4 The Basic Results: Further Tests

Confidence in the results reported in section 6.2 is enlarged by any evidence that they are not artifacts of the tactical choices made in the project's early stages. Two groups of choices can be reconsidered here: the decisions about what individual plant observations to eliminate before computation of the frontier production functions, because of putative data errors or other indications of unsuitability, and the particular technical-efficiency measure selected to serve as the core dependent variable.

The Role of Data-Exclusion Rules

The best instrument for summarizing the effect of the data-editing rules is the number of establishments in the Annual Survey of Manufactures panel that were rejected for each industry. We added this variable to a core regression model to observe its own significance and the effect of its presence on other variables. (There is no need to express the rejection count as a proportion because NOBS, the square root of the number of plants observed, appears as a regressor.[16]) The coefficient of the rejection count itself is not at all significant, and its inclusion has no appreciable effect on the magnitudes or significance levels of most other coefficients. The exception is RSIZE, the relative size (market share) of the median plant, which becomes insignificant as its coefficient drops by two-thirds. This change reflects the finding noted in section 3.3 that the proportion of an industry's plants lost through data exclusions decreased with the total number of its plants. Because technical efficiency has no net regression relationship to the rejection count, this result does not seem to call into question our conclusion about the influence of RSIZE.

We also examined the Spearman correlations between important exogenous variables and the proportion of observations dropped from the analysis (to suggest what coefficients' magnitudes might have been affected). The rejected proportion is negatively correlated with RSIZE, −0.10. It has a strong negative correlation with SD(K/L), perhaps reflecting the fact that our data-editing rules did remove plants with reported levels of capital intensity an extreme number of standard deviations from the industry mean. Had they not been excluded, the interindustry variance of SD(K/L) would have been enlarged and its effect in the regression model changed accordingly. The proportion of observations rejected is strongly correlated with PART, 0.42. This correlation has no obvious explanation in economic behavior or the construction of PART. Thus, data problems may have affected our conclusions about these two regressors. The proportion of observations rejected was significantly lower in industries with both high R&D and high inbound diversification (see table 6.3, equation 4). Thus the conclusion that the negative effect of inbound diversification on efficiency is not greater where R&D spending is important may be overstated because fewer suspicious observations were screened out of the industries with high values of both R&D and inbound diversification.

Related of the question of rejected data is the issue whether any industries as a whole are a priori systematically heterogenous and thus a potential source of distortion in the regression plane. The obvious candidates are the "not elsewhere classified" industries ending in the number 9 in the SIC, which were not excluded from the sample. Our hope was that these industries would appear to be less efficient than well-defined industries, but their presence would not distort the regression plane represented by the core regression model. That hope was in fact realized. The mean value of technical efficiency (EFF) for miscellaneous industries is 0.236, less than the mean of 0.280 for other industries. The difference between means is just significant at 5 percent (one-tail, $t = 1.71$). The zero-order Pearson correlation of a dummy for these industries with EFF (in its log-odds form) is -0.154, and the partial correlation (controlling for NOBS) is -0.095. Including a dummy for these industries in the core regression model changes no other regressor's coefficient by more than 5 percent; for the dummy's coefficient, $t = -1.24$. Thus, the miscellaneous industries do appear to be less efficient than the well-defined ones, but their inclusion does not affect findings about the sample at large.

Alternative Dependent Variables

Recall that the dependent variable used in this chapter—expected technical efficiency (EFF), based on production functions estimated with value added as the dependent variable—was selected from a group of candidates. Others were average technical inefficiency (ATI), lambda (λ), and skewness (S), and production functions were also estimated with gross output as the dependent variable so that each measure could be calculated from the production function estimated with either value added or gross output as the dependent variable. After completing the analysis using only the preferred dependent variable, based on the production function with value added as the dependent variable, we estimated the core model quoted at the beginning of section 6.2 for each alternative combination of technical-efficiency measure and dependent variable in the production function.

Table 6.6 shows the results for all four measures of (in)efficiency calculated for this project. Each measure was obtained from stochastic frontier production functions based on both value added and gross output as dependent variables, although we found grounds for placing greater faith in the measures based on value added. Consider first the equations with value-added–based measures as dependent variables (every other column in table 6.6). With the first column, *EFF(VA)*, taken as the standard of reference, the equation for *S(VA)* shows no sign reversals, and only one coefficient slips to a *t*-statistic less than 1. For *ATI(VA)* the results are similar, with one sign reversal (*PART*), along with one other nonsignificant coefficient. The equation for λ(*VA*) diverges a bit more, with *R&D*'s coefficient significant but with reversed sign. *NOBS* shows the same reversal, but that is consistent with the statistical interpretation we have given to its role in the model (λ's denominator as well as its numerator are affected). For λ(*VA*) all the coefficients whose signs confirm to expectations have significant coefficients.

To assess the results for measures based on gross output, start with a comparison of the first two columns, which report results for *EFF(VA)* and *EFF(GO)*. The two models agree closely except that *VINTM* becomes insignificant with the measure based on gross output. The other models based on gross output diverge somewhat more from the core equation based on *EFF(VA)*. *S(GO)* shows a particularly low level of conformity. One might attribute this to the much larger number of degrees of freedom in the equations for *S*, which is defined for all industries and not just the ones for which *EFF* can be calculated. However, the model for *S(VA)* agrees quite well with that for *EFF(VA)*. Thus, we obtain mixed results for the hypothesis discussed in chapter 4 that the industries for which *EFF(VA)* cannot be calculated in fact have little technical inefficiency. That hypothesis is supported by the *S(VA)* model but not for the *S(GO)* model.

It is inappropriate to reduce the results of table 6.6 to a box score of agreements and disagreements with the model developed around the dependent variable *EFF(VA)*. That is because factors discussed previously warrant assigning more weight to *EFF* than to *ATI*, and *ATI* is preferred to *S* and λ; similarly the evidence in chapter 4 established a strong preference for VA-based over GO-based measures. A comforting feature of table 6.6 is that the divergence of an equation's results from those for *EFF(VA)* clearly increases with the a priori inferiority of its dependent variable to *EFF(VA)* as a measure of technical efficiency. Although no variable's coefficient proves robust to all changes in the dependent variable, in our judgment *NOBS*, *SD(K/L)* and *DIV* emerge almost unscathed. For each of *VINTM*, *R&D*, and

Table 6.6
Effect of alternative dependent variables: Core regression model

Exogenous variable	Measures of efficiency				Measures of inefficiency			
	EFF(VA)	EFF(GO)	S(VA)	S(GO)	ATI(VA)	ATI(GO)	λ(VA)	λ(GO)
NOBS	-0.116	-0.108	-0.001	0.002	0.087	0.092	-0.010	-0.033
	(29.32)	(44.42)	(1.19)	(2.25)	(15.25)	(48.20)	(5.97)	(20.47)
VINTM	-0.013	0.001	-0.001	0.001	0.014	-0.006	0.003	-0.010
	(6.96)	(1.09)	(3.71)	(2.78)	(6.31)	(5.43)	(2.90)	(15.43)
SD(K/L)	-0.013	-0.004	-0.0001	0.0004	0.005	0.001	0.002	0.001
	(12.48)	(7.33)	(0.22)	(1.89)	(4.88)	(2.10)	(2.42)	(4.41)
R&D	-0.044	-0.080	-0.003	-0.005	0.009	0.074	-0.005	-0.014
	(2.77)	(8.03)	(1.24)	(2.46)	(0.60)	(8.53)	(0.64)	(2.50)
RSIZE	3.964	5.195	0.315	-0.100	-3.475	-4.597	-0.730	0.295
	(17.81)	(42.61)	(7.95)	(2.13)	(16.23)	(48.41)	(11.30)	(4.47)
PART	0.837	1.285	0.104	-0.058	0.244	-0.504	-0.230	0.031
	(3.35)	(6.93)	(2.22)	(0.55)	(1.20)	(4.02)	(1.96)	(0.29)
DIV	-0.463	-0.415	-0.054	0.058	0.371	0.232	0.198	0.012
	(8.90)	(9.53)	(4.88)	(2.34)	(7.83)	(5.76)	(7.63)	(0.61)
Constant	1.054	1.744	0.010	-0.084	-1.746	-3.777	0.666	1.244
	(12.08)	(28.01)	(0.60)	(2.74)	(22.84)	(76.90)	(14.60)	(34.46)
$\bar{R}^2$	0.525	0.527	0.057	0.270	0.475	0.514	0.052	0.270
D.f.	277	151	365	359	285	148	294	157

PART, one equation with some claim on credibility reveals a divergent result, but the bulk of the high-credibility models continue to support the findings reported.

Each model reported in table 6.6 was estimated using the maximum number of industries for which all data were available. Thus each was estimated from a different set of observations. We also estimated these models with just that subset of industries for which all data were available for every model. The common number of degrees of freedom is 136. The result, as expected, is typically some slippage in levels of statistical significance, although a few variables become significant with the reduced degrees of freedom. We counted the number of times each variable that is significant at 10 percent or better with the larger number of observations slips below that threshold when the number is reduced. At most one such change occurs for all but two variables: *R&D* losses significance in four of eight possible cases (while gaining it in one), and *PART* loses significance in three cases.

If that conclusion is accepted, one regressor, *R&D*, has its significance substantially compromised by this analysis of alternative dependent variables. *PART* is also called into question by its vulnerability to reduced numbers of observations as well as the results of table 6.6. The other variables survive well enough that we stand with our original conclusions.

Analysis of Residuals

The last step in assessing the results was to examine the residuals from the core model. The lack of a closed theoretical model of technical efficiency warrants an inspection of the largest outliers for common properties that could suggest previously unsuspected influences. In fact, no substantial patterns were detected. Lists of the twenty industries with the largest underestimates and the twenty with the largest overestimates of their efficiency levels appear random with respect to two-digit industries of origin. No difference between these groups is evident in the values of the regressors in the core model. We did conjecture that short-run growth rates (the rate of change of industry shipments from 1976 to 1977) might differ, but the median growth rates of the high- and low-residual industries are in fact about the same.

6.5 Summary

A large number of hypotheses about the determinants of technical efficiency were developed in chapter 5. Because of multicollinearity and problems of missing observations on some exogenous variables, these were tested in a partially sequential fashion by first establishing a core of robust and important determinants and then adding other regressors to this core. The explanatory power of the model is quite high, and many hypotheses were confirmed. They are usefully grouped into families:

1. *Competitive conditions.* Efficiency has no linear relation to the conventional measure of competition among domestic producers—the four-firm concentration ratio. There is, however, a significant quadratic relation that places maximum efficiency around 40 percent, below the range in which oligopolistic behavior appears to become significant. There is weak evidence that collusion (giving rise to antitrust indictments) impairs efficiency, but an inconsistency throws this result into question. Import competition (measured by imports' share of total supply) increases efficiency in industries whose domestic producers are concentrated.

2. *Natural sources of heterogeneity.* Various sources of natural heterogeneity among a market's participants should raise the variance of their revenue/cost ratios but may or may not increase technical inefficiency. In fact we found a number of such sources to affect efficiency. It appears to decrease with product differentiation—specifically differentiation associated with extensive sales-promotion outlays rather than with intrinsic heterogeneity of the product. Efficiency appears lower in geographically fragmented industries, but it is not affected by close involvement with the processing of (potentially heterogenous) primary inputs. It is decreased by the importance of exporting activities because these tend to be spread unevenly among an industry's firms and plants.

3. *Innovation and change.* Previous research showed that estimated efficiency decreases with the importance of vintage effects in the industry's capital stock, and that is confirmed here. It is also reduced by the importance of innovation—apparently due to the uneven distribution of rents from product innovations (incomplete diffusion of process innovations is picked up by the dispersion of capital vintages).[17] We expected efficiency to decrease with fuel intensity because adjustments to the energy shock of 1973 were incomplete as

of 1977. This hypothesis was not confirmed directly, but it appears to account for part of the negative effect on technical efficiency of the dispersion of plants' capital-labor ratios.

4. *Organizational factors.* Several normatively important hypotheses about organizational influences were confirmed. Efficiency decreases with the extent of diversification by enterprises operating plants in the industry (the impairment is especially great for plants managed by firms based in other industries, although their plants in their home industry also suffer). Efficiency increases with the importance of minimum efficient plant scales; large scales apparently increase the absolute downside loss from operating production units inefficiently. Work force organization also affects efficiency, which increases with the incidence of part-time employment (the relation is not entirely robust) and decreases with unionization in industries whose leading plants employ large numbers of workers.[18] Of less normative significance is the decrease of efficiency with the dispersion among the industry's plants of the ratio of nonproduction workers to total employees, reflecting firms' uneven use of separate administrative establishments, maintenance of research and sales force staffs, contracting out of services, and the like.

5. *The order-statistics effect.* The model also includes the square root of the number of (plant) observations used to estimate the frontier production function, as a correction for the "order statistics" relation that was found in chapter 4. This variable is highly significant, and so acceptance of the relationship as purely statistical is necessary for acceptance of the substantive findings related to the number of units present in the industry—effects of concentration and minimum efficient plant size but perhaps also other variables that are correlated with them.

The regression coefficients supply approximate indications of the percentage cost reductions that are attainable by changes (for example, one standard deviation) in the regressors. On this criterion the effects of minimum efficient plant scale and of enterprise diversification are notably strong; the other normatively significant variables more modest.

Several regressors, obtained as by-products of estimation of the frontier production functions, take the form of interplant dispersions of organizational patterns (capital-labor ratio, nonproduction employees' share of employment, share of fuel and energy purchases in materials inputs). We probed further to determine the behavioral forces that enlarge these dispersions. The dispersion of capital-labor ratios increases with the dispersion of wage rates and thus is due partly to factors in the labor market. It also increases with the incidence of part-time employment. It increases with the industry's average capital intensity but is independent of the dispersion of capital vintages. And it seems to be closely associated with the interplant dispersion of fuel usage rates. The dispersion of nonproduction workers' shares of plant-level employment increase, as expected, with the importance of reseach, advertising, and exporting activities for an industry.

The robustness of these results was probed in several ways. We found that the results are largely unaffected by the incidence of the data-editing rules that removed plants from the industry samples prior to estimation of the frontier production functions. The results are not affected by removal of "not elsewhere classified" industries, which in fact do exhibit lower levels of estimated technical efficiency. We reestimated the core regression model with each of the alternative efficiency measures as dependent variables. Some regressors decline in significance; overall part-time employment and the incidence of research activities are the variables that appear the frailest in these tests for robustness.

Efficiency in Large and
Small Establishments

The original design of this project included intensive scrutiny of economies of scale at the establishment's level. Although various factors combined to trim our ambitions along this line, we did address variations in efficiency by size of establishment by calculating separate frontier production functions for large and small establishments in industries with enough plants available for the analysis. After considering the analytical background, we present some computations designed to determine whether any systematic differences exist in the large- and small-plant halves of manufacturing industries, and (if so) to explain why they appear.[1]

The efficiency of small-scale plants is of concern for two reasons. First, they may be subject to diseconomies of small size in suboptimal-scale units, even if their costs are minimized at the scales their operators had chosen. Second, they may display more (or less) technical inefficiency than their large-plant competitors, relative to the frontier production function estimated for their scales of operation. While the resources are lacking for a full joint analysis of these two questions, we can pursue the second while employing some controls for the first.

7.1 Previous Research and Analytical Background

Previous Research

A great deal of research on industrial organization has addressed the efficiency of plant scales in terms of the extent of apparently suboptimal-scale capacity and the reasons that it might exist. The strategy of this research has generally been to assume that suboptimal scales were chosen by intendedly rational managers who might nonetheless be responding to prices or other signals that made their choices of scale privately but not socially optimal. Empirical research from Bain (1956) and Weiss (1964) onward established that while concentrated industries exhibit little suboptimal scale, less concentrated ones may or may not. This result, although it clashes with some hypotheses, agrees with the simple proposition that high concentration usually rests on some form of scale economy and/or first-mover advantage, whether in production facilities or some other activity, that sharply discourages small-scale operations.

Pashigian (1969) and others reported that the extent of suboptimal capacity varies inversely with the cost disadvantage faced by small-scale production units, and Scherer (1973) established the influence of spatial and other cost-based factors on the distribution of actual plant sizes relative to minimum efficient scale. In the same vein, Guth (1971) demonstrated an association between product differentiation and the length of an industry's tail of small-scale units. White (1982) investigated the sizes of industries' fringes of small firms, finding in essence that small units flourish in the absence of the conventional entry barriers. There is only a little evidence (Scherer 1973) to support the hypothesis that price collusion or soft competition improves the viability of suboptimal-scale units.[2] In short, the research on suboptimal-scale production is consistent with rational choices by the units' managers. Small scales are picked because they are expected to yield nonnegative profits; those choices may or may not reflect imperfections in competition associated with collusion or the exploitation of first-mover advantages by a dominant firm or firms.

This evidence is important groundwork for studying technical efficiency in large and small establishments, if only in a negative sense. If profit-seeking decisions seem capable of explaining the scales chosen by small as well as large units, there is no prima facie case for associating small scales with limited rationality, incomplete information, transitional states of industrial infants seeking to grow into large-scale adulthood, or other such explanations that might associate small scale with technical inefficiency. Although such explanations are not precluded, the evidence does not notably support them. Thus, no presumption emerges about the technical efficiency of small relative to large establishments.

Nonetheless, one line of widely replicated empirical evidence contains a result consistent with greater inefficiency in small firms, although it offers no explanation for the pattern. The evidence in question bears on the relation between companies' profit rates and their sizes. Most research of this type was conducted not on competitors in well-defined industries but on broad samples of firms. For such diffuse samples, economic theory suggests no reason that firms' profit rates should vary with their sizes, and in fact no pattern is found by those studies that are free of sampling biases.[3] Nonetheless, studies that paid attention to the variance of profit rates found that it diminishes substantially with size of company (Sherman 1968; Samuels and Smyth 1968). Part of the compression may be due to factors unrelated to efficiency (such as the greater diversification of large firms), but the findings are not inconsistent with technical efficiency showing a positive relation to firm size.

The literature on technical efficiency itself contains little on the relative efficiency of small and large establishments. Only two inter-industry studies seem to have addressed the question, with similar findings. Meller (1976) disaggregated his data on establishments in twenty-one Chilean manufacturing industries into five size classes, the largest having a lower boundary of only 100 employees. Aggregating across all industries, he found more inefficiency in the smallest than in the largest size class, but patterns in individual industries proved quite diverse, with only two showing unambiguous increases of efficiency with scale. Meeusen and van den Broeck (1977b), using a procedure similar to ours, calculated separate frontier production functions in ten two-digit French industries for companies with values of sales falling above and below an arbitrary threshold. They found technical efficiency to be higher in the large-firm than in the small-firm sectors of eight of their ten industries.

Analytical Considerations

Some empirical evidence—these findings on technical efficiency and the data on profit rate dispersions—suggest that efficiency may be lower among the small firms in an industry. We suspect that many economists would guess this outcome, after duly noting the absence of any clear neoclassical foundation. In pursuing possible analytical bases for the relation, we shall continue to neglect the distinction between plants and firms, on the evidence that small firms are normally single-plant operators, and the sizes of plants and firms are positively correlated (without controlling for the extent of multiplant operation). The following analytical considerations apply:

1. *Life cycle and turnover*. Most firms start out small relative to their competitors, and mortality rates in early years are high. There is also evidence that mortality rates and turnover are higher for small than for large firms (Mansfield 1962). Patterns of concentration are consistent with a process whereby a limited number of survivors get out ahead of the pack (Davies and Lyons 1982). These biological processes of growth and mortality in firms are sufficient to explain a pattern whereby small units appear to show more technical inefficiency. In addition to implying that small units should generally appear less efficient, they also suggest that industry characteristics might amplify small-unit inefficiency, and thus enter into a cross-section analysis of relative efficiency. Nominees include the research intensity of the industry (increasing the hazards to which new and small units are exposed) and its recent rate of growth (which increases the proportion of units that are new, by assumption small, and still in a shakedown phase for pursuing normal efficiency) (Hause and Du Rietz 1984).

2. *Entrepreneurship and managerial quality*. The early literature of industrial organization sometimes invoked "cannon-fodder entrepreneurship" to explain the persistence in some markets of fringes of (inefficiently?) small and unprofitable firms. In the era of rational expectations, economists do not easily accept that lotteries will be patronized by classes of persistent losers. Nonetheless, we may give such a story reasonable foundations, even without invoking the assumption that some persons gain nonpecuniary utility from entrepreneurship. Assume that some people are (1) systematically overconfident of their previously untried managerial abilities and (2) unskilled at analyzing information so as to extract unbiased expected values.[4] Assume that large-scale business organizations possess filtering and surveillance mechanisms that limit the access of such individuals to positions in which they hold authority to allocate large quantities of resources. Small businesses, by contrast, require sufficiently small inputs of equity capital that unskilled entrepreneurs can enter with self-supplied funds (and perhaps help from credulous or risk-loving personal investors). Many such entrepreneurs earn subnormal returns and eventually disappear. But as long as the supply is continuously renewed, the typical industry will always contain a stock of cannon fodder. This model both predicts that small-plant sectors will show lower technical efficiency and suggests bases for explaining how this differential might vary among industries. For example, it implies that small units' efficiency should increase with the importance of scale

economies or with capital cost of establishing a viable unit in the industry, both of which intensify the screening of entrepreneurial candidates (Jovanovic 1982).

3. *Measurement error*. Small units may exhibit wider dispersions in the results that they report, whatever the dispersion of their real efficiency levels. An example stems from the the proposition that tax considerations induce excess entrepreneurial withdrawals in small, closely held business (Stigler 1963), so that value added is converted into apparent costs and efficiency seems impaired. The apparent level of technical efficiency would not be affected if entrepreneurs followed this policy uniformly; however, differences in personal circumstances and opportunities surely make the incidence of these withdrawals quite uneven. Other practices could similarly make the dispersion of measured productivity levels decrease with the size of the business.

7.2 Preliminary Analysis of Data

We test the hypothesis that smaller units exhibit lower efficiency and examine certain other patterns in the data before proceeding with an analysis of interindustry differences in the relative efficiency of small units. The efficiency measures utilized are two that were calculated for the full sample: *EFF* (expected technical efficiency) and λ (ratio of the standard deviation of the one-sided to the standard deviation of the symmetrical component of the composed residuals). Because of the close relation between λ and skewness and the odd behavior of average technical inefficiency, *EFF* and λ will suffice. Recall that λ is a measure of inefficiency.

Differences in Medians and Means

Table 7.1 contains descriptive statistics on these variables.[5] Differences in *EFF* support the hypothesis of lower apparent efficiency in small units, but the margin is not large. The median is 15 percent greater in the large-plant sector, the mean 16 percent greater, and the difference in means is statistically significant ($t = 2.93$). These data arise from production functions based on value added as the dependent variable. As a check we examined data on the (much small number of) industries for which *EFF* could be estimated for small and large

Table 7.1
Descriptive statistics: measures of efficiency in large-plant and small-plant sectors

Variable	Small-plant sector	Large-plant sector
Based on value added		
EFF (expected technical efficiency)		
Median	0.26	0.30
Mean	0.28	0.33
Standard deviation	0.14	0.16
Number of observations	191	191
λ (standard deviation of inefficiency/standard deviation of random component)		
Median	0.77	0.77
Mean	0.81	0.81
Standard deviation	0.32	0.34
Number of observations	231	236
Based on gross output		
EFF (expected technical efficiency)		
Median	0.60	0.65
Mean	0.61	0.64
Standard deviation	0.16	0.12
Number of observations	51	51

establishments when gross output is the dependent variable. Again the median is 8 percent greater and the mean 5 percent greater for the large-plant sector. This smaller difference between means in a smaller sample is not statistically significant ($t = 1.10$).

No corresponding difference is observed, however, for the inefficiency measure λ, whose medians and means are the same in the two sectors. Recall that EFF is derived from the standard deviation of the one-sided residuals, while λ is that standard deviation divided by the standard deviation of the symmetrical component of the composed residuals. The differences in EFF indicate that the former component is greater in the small-plant sector, and the absence of a difference in λ shows that the latter must be greater as well. That is consistent with the suggestion that more random noise is likely to be observed in the small-plant sectors, as well as more actual inefficiency.

Because of the significant difference in our main data set (based on value added) and because the lack of a significant difference for λ is theoretically expected, we accept the hypothesis that small-plant sectors show lower technical efficiency.

Correlation Patterns

The correlations among these measures are revealing. The (Spearman) correlation between *EFF* for the industry as a whole and for the small-plant sector (hereafter *EFFS*) is 0.803, greater than the correlation of *EFF* with its large-plant counterpart (*EFFL*), 0.700, and considerably greater than the correlation between *EFFS* and *EFFL*, 0.400. *EFF* is an unweighted efficiency measure, and these correlations show that its interindustry variation reflects the pattern of small establishments even more than that of large ones.[6] These relations can be approached by regressing *EFF* on *EFFS* and *EFFL*. For value added we obtain:

$$EFF = -0.028 + 0.432\ EFFS + 0.298\ EFFL \qquad\qquad \bar{R}^2 = 0.76.$$
$$(2.8)\qquad (15)\qquad\quad (11)$$

The coefficient of *EFFS* is 45 percent larger than that for *EFFL*.[7] We wondered whether the efficiency of an industry is positively associated with the similarity of efficiency levels in its subsectors. The difference *EFFS − EFFL* and the absolute difference |*EFFS − EFFL*| were calculated and their correlations with industry-wide *EFF* examined; those values (0.044 and −0.056) are not statistically significant.

We were concerned that the theoretical grounds for expecting efficiency to increase with unit size associate inefficiency with absolute smallness, while the mean sizes of the small- and large-plant samples vary freely from industry to industry (that is, each industry's plants were ranked by size and divided around the median plant). For each industry a measure was obtained of the fraction of establishments that in 1977 employed twenty or more workers (*FEB*). If absolute (small) size is important for the difference between *EFFS* and *EFFL*, then *FEB* should be positively correlated with *EFFS*. The correlation is 0.114, significant at 9 percent; *FEB* is uncorrelated with *EFFL* (0.040). Relative small-plant efficiency and absolute smallness thus are at least weakly linked.

Because of the pervasive importance of *EFF*'s relation to the number of observations underlying the frontier production function, we ascertained that this same relation holds for *EFFS* and *EFFL*. When each of these three efficiency measures is regressed on the number of

Table 7.2
Industry-wide, small-plant, and large-plant efficiency as explained by core regression model

Exogenous variable	Efficiency measure		
	EFF	EFFS	EFFL
NOBS	−0.116	−0.087	−0.090
	(29.32)	(28.23)	(14.33)
VINTM	−0.013	−0.008	−0.003
	(6.73)	(4.69)	(1.32)
SD(K/L)	−0.013	−0.011	−0.016
	(12.48)	(9.98)	(20.12)
R&D	−0.044	−0.025	−0.018
	(2.77)	(1.78)	(1.04)
DIV	−0.463	−0.176	−0.577
	(8.90)	(3.97)	(11.73)
RSIZE	3.964	2.446	2.793
	(17.81)	(24.74)	(22.55)
PART	0.837	0.456	0.047
	(3.35)	(2.52)	(0.26)
Constant	1.054	0.652	1.054
	(12.08)	(11.24)	(13.07)
$\bar{R}^2$	0.525	0.336	0.403
d.f.	277	195	200

observations giving rise to *EFF*, its square and its square root, the regression coefficients and goodness of fit are quite similar for the three.

Regression Analysis

The last preliminary test is to regress *EFFS* and *EFFL* on the core model of the determinants of *EFF* reported in chapter 6. The model was estimated for the maximum number of industries for which all variables were available, so each equation covers a slightly different sample. The regressors are the same industry-wide observations utilized in chapter 6. The results are shown in table 7.2, in which White's correction for heteroskedasticity has been employed.

The equation for *EFF*, included for comparison, is the one reported in section 6.2. The coefficients of *NOBS* and *SD(K/L)* are similar in magnitude and significance across the three models, and *RSIZE* seems to wield no differential effect. Interesting differences appear for other variables. *PART* is a significant determinant of *EFFS* but not *EFFL*; we expect small plants more readily to utilize the flexibility of part-time workers. Similarly *DIV*, the incidence of corporate diversification, should have its negative effect on efficiency in large plants; although we cannot directly associate plants with the product diversity of the owning firms, it is well established that large firms are more diversified and that large and multibusiness companies operate larger plants than single-plant firms. Indeed while *DIV*'s coefficient is negative in all three models, it is three times as large and much more significant for *EFFL* than for *EFFS*. We would expect the negative effect of *EFF* of *R&D* to be greater in the small-plant sectors because most small units do not undertake R&D, and studies of intraindustry diffusion typically find larger units in the lead. Indeed *R&D*'s coefficient is negative and significant for *EFFS* but not for *EFFL*. Perhaps surprisingly *VINTM* exerts a stronger influence in the small-plant sectors. It may be that old capital is concentrated in small plants that operate below present-day minimum efficient scale. However, because of the persuasive evidence that capital intensity increases with plant scale within industries, the vintage dispersion's effect should be more evident among the large plants.

7.3 Determinants of Differences in Small and Large Plants' Efficiency

We proceed to a regression analysis of the differences between efficiency levels in industries' large- and small-plant sectors. The dependent variable may be either the simple difference,

$$EFFD = EFFL - EFFS,$$

or a normalized version of the same,

$$EFFND = (EFFL - EFFS)/(EFFL + EFFS).$$

Theory does not provide refined guidance about possible regressors, and the following conjectures should be regarded as exploratory.

Hypotheses about Determinants

We have suggested two avenues for explaining *EFFD*: differences among industries in firms' life cycles or hazard rates and in access to the industry by entrepreneurs with untried and possibly inadequate skills. Each of these approaches suggests several regressors, and others are invoked by the results of chapter 6 and table 7.2.

The life-cycle approach suggests that *EFFD* should increase with attributes of the industry that raise the uncertainty surrounding the returns expected by new and small firms. We know that the importance of intangible capital to an industry, reflected in the incidence of research and development and large-scale sales promotion outlays, is positively associated with the dispersion of the fortunes of small competitors (e.g., Stonebraker 1976). One appropriate predictor is company-financed research and development outlay as a fraction of sales, *R&D*, used in chaper 6.[8] The most suitable predictor based on the importance of customer goodwill assets is probably media advertising outlays as a proportion of sales, *MADS*, or simply the total advertising-sales ratio, *ADS*.[9] A third possibility is the measure of product differentiation based on principal-component analysis, *PC1*, employed in chapter 6. It indicates negatively the importance of media advertising and the unimportance of the individual purchase to the buyer; positively it indicates the complexity of the product's attributes. *EFFD* should be positively related to *MADS* or *ADS*, negatively related to *PC1*.

Some sources of differential uncertainty in business units' success rates operate more strongly on the larger units. One identified by the results of chapter 6 is involvement in export markets. Exporting activities apparently involve greater fixed costs as well as uncertainties than selling to domestic customers. As a result, they are concentrated among an industry's larger plants and firms and should thus reduce the apparent efficiency of large units relative to the smaller competitors with less average involvement in export sales (Caves 1986). The variable employed is the ratio of industry exports to shipments, averaged over 1972–1976 (*XS*). In summary, considerations of life cycle and uncertainty suggest that *EFFD* should increase with *R&D*, *MADS*, and/or *ADS* and decrease with *XS*.

Although we lack systematic descriptive evidence on firms' life cycles and mortality rates at their various stages, it seems likely that the failure rate for recently founded firms is high in most industries. New firms are also likely to start out small (unless minimum operating scales are sharply constrained by technology). Finally, the rate of entry of new firms to a market is known to be closely related to its rate of growth (Hause and Du Rietz 1984). Putting these facts together, we obtain the prediction that the more rapidly an industry has been growing, the larger is its proportion of new, small firms subject to high rates of infant mortality and hence (before they expire) to low technical efficiency. Therefore we expect that *EFFD* will increase with the rate of real-output growth over the preceding decade, 1968–1977 (denoted *GROW*).

We also suggested that *EFFD* might decrease with the importance of factors denying access to an industry for unskilled and inexperienced entrepreneurs. The results of table 7.2 implied that this effect is captured by *RSIZE*, which indicates the relative size (share of market) achieved by the median plant, assumed to be correlated with the (unobserved) cost penalties incurred by smaller units.[10] If the capital market importantly serves to head off unskilled entrepreneurs, a better specification might be *KSIZE*, the capital required to fund the industry's median-scale plant. Other plausible specifications include the absolute size (dollar shipments) made by the median-sized plant (*PSIZE*) or the absolute sizes (shipments) of the largest companies operating in the industry (*COSIZE*). Because each of these variables suggests the presence of deterrents to unskilled entrepreneurs in the industry's small-plant sector, their effect on *EFFD* should be negative.

Additional influences on *EFFD* include any determinants of *EFF* from chapter 6 not covered by the hypotheses just listed but expected to exert differential effects on large and small units. One conspicuous candidate is *DIV*, enterprise-level diversification. Plants controlled by multiplant and multi-industry firms are known on average to be the larger ones operating in an industry,[11] so the adverse effect of corporate diversification operates more strongly in the large-plant sector, hence depressing *EFFD* and *EFF*. We shall check the respective strength of *DIV's* components, inbound (*COVE*) and outbound (*SPECE*) diversification. Another influence on *EFF* that might also affect *EFFD* is the incidence of part-time employment, *PART*. Large plants are generally believed to gain scale economies at some expense in flexibility, including the ease of handling diverse working schedules (as well as utilizing the talents of individuals less congenial to regimented working arrangements). *EFFD* should then decrease with *PART*.

Statistical Results

Table 7.3 sets forth the principal results obtained from testing these hypotheses. The dependent variable in the reported equations is

Table 7.3
Determinants of differences between efficiency levels in large-plant and small-plant sectors

Exogenous variable	Equation				
	1	2	3	4	5
R&D	0.020	0.019	0.032	0.032	0.017
	(5.74)	(5.40)	(11.49)	(12.23)	(6.82)
MADS				0.003	
				(1.89)	
PC1					−0.007
					(2.48)
XS			−0.004	−0.003	−0.002
			(6.08)	(5.68)	(4.38)
GROW			−0.045		
			(3.77)		
RSIZE	−1.667[a]	−1.720[a]	−1.248[a]		
KSIZE				−0.180	−0.029
				(17.78)	(1.96)
DIV	−0.108		−0.030[a]	−0.050	−0.109
	(9.12)			(6.38)	(15.85)
COVE		−0.145			
		(7.28)			
SPECE		−0.066			
		(2.40)			
Constant	0.108	0.109	0.071	0.052	0.090
	(14.28)	(11.16)	(11.00)	(8.64)	(20.14)
$\bar{R}^2$	0.043	0.039	0.044	0.027	0.050

a. The heteroskedasticity-corrected standard error took a low value that implies a noncredibly high t-statistic.

EFFD, as the normalized variable EFFND gives slightly less significant results throughout, and there is no compelling reason for the normalization. Heteroskedasticity-consistent standard errors are reported.[12]

Several models are quoted in table 7.3 in order to display the effect of variables that provide alternative embodiments of certain hypotheses. Consider first those addressing hazard rates that should differ between large and small units. R&D takes the predicated positive coefficient that is highly significant and robust to specification changes. That is, the hazards confronting small units appear relatively greater in innovative industries. Media advertising (MADS) has the same effect (equation 4), although the significance level is only 5 per-cent (one-tail test). That result is confirmed by the significant negative coefficient of *PC1* in equation 5; *PC1* negatively reflects heavy sales promotion of homogeneous products and positively reflects goods' structural differentiation.[13] The overall advertising-sales ratio (*ADS*) as an alternative to these two is not significant.

Two other sources of differential hazard were tested. The exports-shipments ratio (*XS*) was expected to affect large units dispro-portionally, and in equations 3, 4, and 5 it takes a negative coefficient, significant at 1 percent. We expected the recent growth of industry output to be positively related to differential efficiency because it would enlarge the proportion of young, small firms with high mortal-ity rates. However, in equation 3 *GROW* contrarily takes a negative coefficient that is significant at 1 percent. We do not find a persuasive counter-hypothesis to interpret this result, but differential adjust-ment costs of expansion by established large plants is a possibility suggested by the approach of Hause and Du Rietz (1984).[14]

Several variables were employed to control for the factors screen-ing out optimistic and/or modestly talented entrepreneurs and thereby raising the efficiency of small plants. The coefficient of the most appropriate variable, the capital cost of a plant of minimum effi-cient scale (*KSIZE*), is significant with the expected negative sign in equations 4 and 5, although its significance level differs greatly be-tween them. *RSIZE*, the output of a minimum-efficient-scale plant as a fraction of the size of the market, is highly significant in equations 1 and 2. Other unit-size measures obtain less statistical significance, in line with their lesser theoretical appropriateness. We do not claim to have identified precisely the screening mechanism that helps the effi-ciency levels of small units, but the results seem strongly consistent with the existence of some such mechanism.

Two variables that affect industries' overall efficiency levels were hypothesized to affect large and small units differentially. The nega-tive effect of enterprise diversification (*DIV*)—because multi-industry firms tend to operate large plants—is illustrated in equations 1 and 3. In equation 2 *DIV* is separated into its components measuring control of the industry's plants by outside firms (*COVE*) and involvement of firms based in this industry with diversified plants (*SPECE*). Each component's coefficient is negative and significant. Inbound diversi-fication is more significant, as it was in chapter 6, but the coefficients indicate that outbound diversification exerts the larger influence.

While we cannot reject the hypothesis that the impairment of efficiency by diversified enterprises is concentrated in industries' large-plants sectors, we found no evidence that the incidence of part-time employment proves more beneficial in small-plant sectors; *PART* (not shown in table 7.3) is not significant, and its sign varies with the model's specification.

It is no surprise that our ability to explain *EFFD* is rather modest. The dependent variable is surely a very noisy measure, and the theoretical resources available to explain it are modest. Although each equation is significant overall at the 5 percent level, the proportion of variance explained is small.

7.4 Summary

We extended the analysis of technical efficiency to the differential performance of small and large plants within each industry by dividing each industry with data available on sixty or more plants into halves and estimating technical efficiency separately for the larger and smaller halves of its plants.

Procedural and substantive reasons supported this extension. On the procedural side, our industry-wide measures of technical efficiency are not weighted by plants' sizes, giving rise to a natural concern about the degree to which the results of chapter 6 depend on conditions prevailing among small plants. Indeed, industry-wide efficiency levels proved somewhat more strongly associated with small-plant than with large-plant efficiency patterns. Substantively we sought to address some questions arising in the theory of the firm and the empirical literature of industrial organization on the relative efficiency of large and small plants. The small-plant sectors were expected to appear less efficient for several reasons. They include the newer units that should show relatively high variance in their performance and are also disadvantageously affected by factors that increase the hazards to business units overall (such as the prevalence of innovation). They include any fringe of unskilled entrepreneurs with high probabilities of failure and who would be filtered out (by the financial markets or other monitors) of activities that require large scales of operation. Measurement errors may also be involved. Expected technical efficiency (our basic measure) is indeed lower in the small-plant sectors. The difference is statistically significant although not large.

These reasons for expecting inferior small-unit efficiency can be tested directly because their incidence should differ from industry to industry. The dependent variable employed in the regression analysis is the difference between expected technical efficiency in an industry's large-plant and small-plant subsectors. An interindustry analysis failed to reject the influence of several variables suggested by the considerations of greater rates of failure in small units and varying accessibility for unskilled entrepreneurs. As for the first class of factors, the superiority of large units' efficiency increases with the importance of research and development outlays in the industry and with the importance of media advertising. It decreases with the importance of exporting activities because these risky operations tend to be concentrated in industries' larger units. Contrary to expectations, we found that rapid growth of the industry in the preceding decade decreases the relative efficiency of large plants; because growth promotes entry and entrants start out small and suffer high mortality rates, a positive relation was anticipated.

Several competing variables were employed to test the presence of filters that would exclude unskilled or overly optimistic entrepreneurs who are would-be entrants. The capital cost of a plant of minimum efficient scale, our preferred variable, is indeed significant and correctly signed although less significant than the minimum-efficient-scale output as a fraction of industry shipments. We conclude that some such filtering mechanism exists but that we have not discriminated successfully among several competing formulations of it.

The differential efficiency of large plants is reduced by the prevalence of corporate diversification. This result provides important confirmation of the finding of chapter 6 that diversification is hostile to technical efficiency. While the inefficiency cannot be tied specifically to the plants operated by multi-industry enterprises, we do know that such firms tend to operate large plants; the negative effect of multi-industry operation on the relative efficiency of large plants therefore tightens the net of circumstantial evidence.

The analysis of small and large establishments reported in this chapter only scratches the surface, we note with regret. At the inception of this project, we planned to analyze in some detail the properties of the estimated production functions, including a comparison of the similarity of those estimated for large and small units separately, as well as a close analysis of their implications for efficient scales and the penalties of suboptimal scales. That analysis was truncated and confined to the inquiry reported in this chapter due to a number of mainly budgetary constraints. These grew from the fact that the Bureau of the Census was unable to transmit the results of estimating the frontier production functions to us in machine-readable form. The considerable key-punching expense that would be required to return the coefficient sets to machine-readable form for further analysis has not been affordable. Specifically, we could not enrich this chapter (as we would have liked) with reports on the similarity of the production functions estimated for large and small units.

8 Technical Efficiency and Productivity Growth

The method of measuring industrial efficiency used in this study has proved itself reasonably well, in the sense of confirming numerous and diverse hypotheses about the factors that should determine efficiency. If that conclusion is accepted, the many consequences of industries' diverse levels of efficiency become natural candidates for research. The spurious components of measured inefficiency (such as product differentiation) are apparently stable and themselves have no effects on economic behavior. However, genuine inefficiencies offer potential pecuniary rewards for those who can devise ways to eliminate them, and so we do not expect them necessarily to remain constant over time. A good example is the negative effect of corporate diversification on efficiency, which offers a compelling explanation for the wave of management buy outs and corporate rationalizations seen in the 1980s (Ravenscraft and Scherer 1987).

In this chapter we take an initial step toward exploring the consequences of technical inefficiency by inquiring whether static inefficiency interacts with and affects an industry's rate of productivity growth. Specifically, does a low level of efficiency impair an industry's ability to attain productivity growth? This question, like many others about the causes of technical inefficiency, lacks a strong theoretical foundation; however, it raises issues of sufficient potential importance to warrant an exploratory inquiry.

8.1 Hypotheses about Technical Efficiency and Productivity Growth

Efficiency and Productivity Growth: Individual Organizations

The hypothesis that inefficiency in the static sense is hostile to productivity growth has a plausible basis in organizational behavior. An organizational coalition that cannot manage its internal allocations so as to obtain the most output from its inputs is by definition failing to adopt superior arrangements that are known and in use in rival organizations. Whatever the source of its infirmity, such an organization should not reach out with alacrity for new production arrangements that are untried or that it must discover itself.

A conceptual underpinning for this hypothesis is best found outside the neoclassical theory of the firm, among the various elements of evolutionary and organizational approaches to the firm. A complex organization develops a set of routines that draw on decentralized knowledge and suffice as responses to the range of disturbances that ordinarily intrude. Problem solving is itself routinized within this context, but the formulation of a problem and the range of solutions contemplated themselves depend on the existing organizational structure. Major changes in the unit's operations upset the existing repertory and the ambient coordination process. Hence they are sought and embraced only when a stimulus—threat or opportunity—reaches some critical mass. A firm that is technically inefficient but viable may score poorly on productivity gains for a number of reasons. An inefficient firm may have a higher threshold for its perception of threats and opportunities or a lower level of aspiration. Its routines may represent something of a stalemated truce among unresolved conflicting interests, increasing the perceived costs of changing the routines and impairing its agility and flexibility. The repertory of routines available for recombining into new and more productive configurations may itself be more limited than in efficient firms.[1]

This line of reasoning is not conventional wisdom, but it is consistent with our evidence on technical efficiency and claims some explanatory force in other contexts. Students of business administration frequently accept the notion that some business firms are excellently managed and that their excellence is persistent, if not eternal.[2] Seeking to explain differences among industrial countries in long-run rates of output growth, some economists have urged that societies with widely prevalent rent-preserving contracts and institutions are prone to slow growth because growth inevitably causes redistributive changes (Olson 1982). In short, to the extent that technical inefficiency turns out to result from suboptimization by organizational coalitions, it seems plausible that the failing should affect both their static and dynamic efficiency levels.

Efficiency, Productivity Growth, and Market Interactions

We must recall, however, that in this study the industry, not the firm or business unit, is the unit of observation. The hypothesis of a positive relation between static and dynamic efficiency in the individual unit cannot yield industry-level predictions until we can consider the equilibrating process among directly competing units that vary in their levels of technical efficiency. The technical inefficiency we measure stems from the dispersion of efficiency levels among plants classified to an industry. The accuracy of the measurement depends, roughly, on the presence of enough efficient units to define a production frontier from which the others' shortcomings can be detected. The productivity growth rate of an industry can be regarded as a (size-weighted) average of the productivity growth rates attained by all the units operating within it. If inefficient firms are unprogressive and efficient competitors' productivity growth rates are unaffected by their sluggard rivals, the industry's rate of productivity growth will be pulled down. This assumed independence may not hold, however, because opportunities missed by inefficient firms raise the benefits to efficient firms of seizing those opportunities. Just as efficient firms profitably expand and displace their inefficient rivals, unprogressiveness by the inefficient deepens their inefficiency and raises the value of the displacement opportunity. Unprogressiveness born of inefficiency at the firm level aggregates to an industry-level relation only if not fully offset by additional opportunities created for productivity gains by the (more) efficient firms.

The issue of appropriability and incentives in the literature on innovation nicely illustrates the mechanism of offsetting opportunities for efficient firms. Suppose that an industry, consisting of half "efficient" and half "inefficient" production units, gains access to a productivity-raising innovation. In order to obtain the productivity gain, each unit must undertake a substantial investment. Each manager conjectures on the expected profitability of adopting the innovation. One datum entering into the calculus is the expected rate of adoption by competing units because it influences the rate at which the industry's market price is expected to decline due to the expansion of output by successful innovators who obtain lower variable costs.[3] Inefficient units, on the hypothesis advanced, suffer infirmities for profitably using the innovation that make them laggard adopters. But their very tardiness raises the payout to prompt adoption by the efficient units because (assuming that efficient new units cannot quickly enter the industry) it limits the rate of intraindustry diffusion for the innovation and the speed with which total output expands and the market price declines. At this level of generality, nothing tells us whether the appropriability advantage gained by efficient firms would suffice to offset the lag of the inefficient ones. Indeed we cannot even say whether the magnitude of the offset should be sensitive to the proportion of inefficient and efficient firms, so long as both are present. Related—and equally indeterminate— conclusions arise if the issue is framed in static terms of the opportunities for efficient firms to displace inefficient ones, raising industry productivity simply by changing the weights in the weighted average.

Empirical evidence is not much help in settling the issue. The literature on producer concentration indicates sufficiently high stability over time for the typical industry that little room exists for major tides of displacement of the inefficient or unprogressive. Yet industries with high rates of productivity growth tend to be, and perhaps to become, concentrated.[4] Once more we are left with the conclusion that inefficient units create incentives for their own displacement, and inefficient and unprogressive firms strengthen that incentive; the existence of a positive industry-level relation between technical efficiency and productivity growth is compromised but not precluded.

Might it not be compromised at all? Could the unprogressiveness of inefficient units fail to create an incentive for enhanced productivity-raising incentives by the more efficient? The Carnegie school would seem to admit this possibility. If firms operate with considerable ignorance of the opportunity sets ultimately open to them, their pursuit of innovation and productivity-raising opportunities depends in part on actions taken by rival firms and the perceived threats and opportunities they reveal. The fewer the "progressive" rivals, the less is a firm (of any given efficiency) exposed to evidence indicating the extent and nature of more productive configurations of activities. While empirical evidence supports no such extreme limitations on the propensities of firms to scan for productivity-raising opportunities, scrambles for productivity-raising improvements by important U.S. industries facing unanticipated increases of international competition are hardly inconsistent with this story.[5]

This analysis of industry-level relations between technical efficiency and productivity gains has not been decisive, but it does support this conclusion: if one accepts the hypothesis that an individual inefficient firm in isolation is likely to be unprogressive, no empirically supported theory precludes that association's holding at the level of the industry, even after more efficient firms have seized the opportunities thereby made available to them.[6]

Effect of Productivity Growth on Inefficiency

While we shall be testing the hypothesis that industries' levels of technical efficiency in 1977 affected their productivity growth during the following decade, the findings of chapter 6 warn that causation might run in the other direction. Suppose that productivity growth rates of industries show substantial persistence, due (say) to exogenous and long-lasting differences in technological opportunity. Suppose that productivity growth affects technical efficiency as measured by means of the frontier production function. Then the time structure of our test would not guarantee against picking up a relation between pre-1977 productivity growth and 1977 technical efficiency, if pre- and post-1977 productivity growth are sufficiently correlated. Fortunately the sign of the expected effect of productivity growth on technical efficiency (as measured) is opposite to that hypothesized for the effect of efficiency on productivity growth: past and current productivity growth should reduce the level of apparent technical efficiency. Empirically no statistically significant relationship was found in chapter 6 between productivity growth between 1968 and 1977 and technical efficiency in 1977, although some of the expected negative effect seems to feed through two other variables. One of these is research and development spending, which serves partly as an investment in productivity gains. We found that an industry's technical efficiency (as measured) decreases with its R&D intensity. The other variable is the dispersion of the capital-labor ratios of the industry's plants, which negatively affects technical efficiency and itself is positively affected by productivity growth.[7] Thus the direction of causation should not be a problem in the analysis that follows.

8.2 Estimating the Effects of Efficiency on Productivity Growth

We now develop a statistical model to test whether an industry's productivity growth increases with its technical efficiency. The cross-section test will not prove as comprehensive as that in chapters 5 and

6, for two reasons: the paucity of statistical resources and the lack of any strong operational model of the determinants of differences in industries' rates of productivity growth.

Consider the problem of data sources first. Total factor productivity growth is not available for manufacturing industries disaggregated to the level that we require, forcing resort to labor productivity. Two sources of labor productivity growth rates are available, one emanating from the U.S. Bureau of Labor Statistics (BLS) and the other from the U.S. International Trade Administration (ITA). We turned first to the BLS data (U.S. Bureau of Labor Statistics 1979, 1986) because of certain attractive properties, such as corrections for changes in finished-good inventories, use of current-weighted price indexes, and appropriate adjustments to employment data. However, the BLS data do not cover all manufacturing industries; matching them to the industries for which measures of technical efficiency are available, we obtained only eighty-eight observations, with the lost observations looking distinctly nonrandom. Furthermore, when the research began, they were available only to 1984 (1983 for some industries). While BLS productivity growth measures for 1977–1984 were kept in play, we centered our attention on the ITA data, which are available through 1986 and cover all manufacturing industries. This data base is used to produce the annual publication *U.S. Industrial Outlook*; it includes real shipments, employment, exports, and imports for four-digit SIC industries, as well as other variables derived from the *Annual Survey of Manufactures*. Nearly quadrupling the number of industries seemed amply worth the lack of certain minor refinements in the ITA data. Specifically the dependent variable from this source, *PR*, is the annualized rate of growth of real shipments per employee between 1977 and 1986.

Control Variables: Growth, Innovation, and Experience

We now face the problem of modeling the determinants of industries' rates of productivity growth. Because productivity growth flows from diverse factors, including improved input qualities, skills, and organizational arrangements, we lack focused theories that can support an integrated empirical model. Instead the quest for a reasonably complete model must be catch-as-catch-can. Previous research on productivity-growth rates (for example, Kendrick 1973, chap. 6) has emphasized two variables. One of these is the rate of output growth, taken to represent the growth of the market determined exogenously from the demand side. Market growth, according to "Verdoorn's law" (Bairam 1987), bestirs productivity gains by inducing more investment in innovation, promoting economies of scale, spreading fixed costs, allowing a finer division of labor, and so forth. While the data always seem to confirm this relationship, the tests could well be spurious. That is because rapid productivity growth lowers the product's relative price and increases the quantity bought, so that the statistical relation could reflect causation running in either direction (Caves 1970). Furthermore the change in output is one component of the measurement of productivity changes, so that measurement errors generate a spurious positive relation. The bias and misspecification that can arise in testing the Verdoorn relation do not greatly concern us, given the chief objective of testing the effect of technical efficiency on productivity growth. Therefore the model will be estimated both including and excluding RQ, the annualized rate of growth of deflated shipments of the industry between 1977 and 1986.

The second variable that has received attention as a determinant of productivity growth is the rate of innovation in relevant technologies and the ambient level of technological opportunity. The importance of controlling for technological opportunity is clear from investigations of the effect of industry competition on innovative input or output (Scherer 1965), and the effect of R&D on productivity growth has been established (Terleckyj 1974). The two control variables utilized here rest on the substantial empirical evidence that links productivity growth to innovation and identifies the structural determinants for opportunities to raise productivity or generate innovations.

The first control is the industry's ratio of company-financed research and development expenditures to sales, taken from the Federal Trade Commission Line of Business data for the year 1976.[8] This is the variable $R&D$, employed as a determinant of technical efficiency. The FTC data are available only for the mid-1970s, which precluded measuring the variable over the whole period for which productivity growth is observed. Although an industry's productivity growth depends on innovative efforts made in other industries (for which we lack data), it also depends on its own R&D outlays.[9]

The other control used to indicate an industry's productivity growth potential is the amount of new capital equipment installed, a channel by which its productivity is enhanced by embodied R&D and innovation in supplier industries. We therefore obtained for each industry the ratio of gross capital expenditure to employment for the years 1977–1986 taken together. Besides controlling for the industry's access to and use of embodied new technology, this variable may help correct for the misspecification in using labor productivity rather than total factor productivity as the dependent variable. Both the research intensity ($R\&D$) and investment intensity ($\triangle K/L$) variables should exert positive influences on productivity growth, along with technical efficiency (EFF).

A source of productivity gains somewhat independent of those already recognized is the learning curve, which rests on skills honed and equipment and procedures tuned with the cumulation of output experience and/or time. Measures of learning-curve slopes are not available for broad samples of manufacturing industries, but the results of Lieberman (1984) identify important predictors. These include, besides variables already specified here, the capital intensity and scale of the production process. Other things equal, learning appears to accumulate faster in industries with technology that requires large-scale units and places substantial cost penalties on small scales.[10] The variable employed is familiar from the research literature on industrial organization, MES/CDR, a measure of minimum efficient scale (relative to the market) adjusted for the productivity disadvantage of suboptimal-scale operation (see the Appendix for details). PR should increase with MES/CDR, although the gap between concept and statistical proxy makes the hypothesis more conjectural than those preceding.

Import Competition and Productivity Growth

Because of the large effects of changing international competition on the structure of U.S. manufacturing industries and the evidence (chapter 6) of favorable effects of import competition on technical efficiency, we also investigated whether productivity growth has been affected by the incursion of foreign competitors on U.S. product markets. The relation of productivity growth to disturbances in international trade is a large subject associated with the process of changes in a nation's comparative-advantage structure. The neoclassical approach to that relation assumes that industries' relative productivity levels (like the nation's comparative-advantage structure) are determined by fundamental attributes of technology and factor supplies and, by extension, that changes in relative productivity stem from these same fundamentals. While the idea is now popular that comparative advantage may to some extent reflect will, desire, and public policy, that belief (and the strategic models to which it leads) wins little support from systematic empirical evidence. Nor has it been confronted with the older idea that international competition (especially for concentrated domestic industries) may provide an especially potent stimulus for innovation and change.

Suppose that productivity growth reflects the sum of intendedly rational decisions by managers and others in an industry to adopt new technologies, make best use of the changing stock of available inputs, and respond efficiently to changes in the structure of demand. When a national industry that we observe faces rivalry from imports, changes in import competition (think of them as changes in the home-delivered price of foreign supplies) shift the parameters governing resource use in ways that affect the industry's productivity (ratio of real output to real inputs). Consider these links:

1. *Specific factors.* Assume that industries are purely competitive and that each makes use of factors of production that are specialized or specific to the industry (at least in the short run). Then each industry operates on a rising supply curve. Any contraction in the face of lower prices of competing imports should raise labor productivity if labor is not the specific factor because more intensive use is made of the specific factor.[11] Thus, import penetration and productivity growth could be positively related for reasons resting on a very spare characterization of industries' organization.

2. *Product differentiation.* The past decade's research on monopolistic competition and international trade (Helpman 1981; Krugman 1981) has established that production scales and thus industry average productivity levels may be affected by an industry's exposure to international trade. At a less abstract level, competitive processes in differentiated-product markets have been found both theoretically and empirically to make the mixture of "varieties" or "brands" offered by an industry depend on its international competitive position. The computable general equilibrium model of Harris (1984), for example, showed that Canada's protection of differentiated and imperfectly competitive manufacturing industries exacts a substantial cost in economic welfare that manifests itself as impaired real productivity in such industries. This model implies that tariff reduction (or, for that matter, other changes reducing the real delivered price of competing imports) will induce reorganizations that enlarge the scale

of production for the typical (surviving) variety and thereby raise productivity. An analysis of Canadian industries' adjustments to international disturbances in the 1970s found that tariff reductions led to increases in industries' capital expenditures, a necessary (but not sufficient) condition for rationalizing the product lines and brand scales offered by domestic producers (Caves 1987). These rationalizing changes could account for a positive relation between import competition (import penetration, say) and productivity growth.

3. *Imported technology*. Many important productivity-raising innovations take place outside the United States and diffuse to domestic producers through various channels, including imported capital goods, licensed technologies, and intangible flows of nonproprietary information. These sources of gain are controlled incompletely if at all by the variables $R\&D$ and $\triangle K/L$. If innovations are first adopted near the site of their discovery, as the evidence indicates, they will tend to shift the supply curve of importables and increase actual imports. A positive association between increasing imports and productivity growth could therefore proxy these unobserved sources of imported productivity gains.

4. *Productivity-raising investments*. Policymakers often urge industries pressed by import competition to invest in order to raise their productivity. However, apart from the product-line rationalization, the expected returns from ordinary sorts of productivity-raising investments are unlikely to be elevated when import competition grows tougher. The expected values of quasi-rents flowing from such investments are likely to be reduced by any change that portends a lower product price and a smaller market accessible to domestic producers. Increases in import competition have this withering effect if they represent secular shifts in comparative advantage (and not one-shot changes or temporary bursts associated with disturbances to the real exchange rate). This consideration could account for a negative relation between import penetration of domestic markets and domestic industries' rates of productivity growth.

In conclusion, several distinct mechanisms with inconsistent sign predictions stand ready to explain how changes in import competition and in productivity growth might be related. We include among the determinants of productivity growth the variable $\triangle MS$, which is the ratio of imports to the sum of imports and competing domestic product shipments for 1986, minus the corresponding ratio for 1977.

Adjustments to Measured Technical Efficiency

The technical-efficiency measure included in the model (*EFF*) is that employed as a dependent variable in chapter 6. The analysis of chapter 6 makes clear, however, that the variable embraces certain spurious elements that are not properly associated with the hypothesis set out in section 8.1. A spurious component is one associated with an exogenous influence that affects technical efficiency as measured but is independent of the bahavior and allocative choices of actual firms. This criterion does not cleanly indicate which variables employed as regressors in chapter 6 should be flagged for removal because some represent mixtures of spurious components and opportunities for behavioral inefficiency (*R&D* is an example). We chose to apply the criterion narrowly, removing from *EFF* only the following influences:

NOBS = square root of the number of observations used in estimating the frontier production function.
RAD   = radius within which 80 percent of industry shipments were made (measure of market localization).
RAW   = proportion of inputs originating from primary sectors.
PC1   = first principal component indicating structural product differentiation.

In chapter 6 each of these except *RAW* proved statistically significant. We regressed *EFF* (in its log-odds form) on these variables and took residuals to form the variable *EFFAJ*. *PR* should increase with *EFF* or *EFFAJ*.[12]

An assumption underlying the hypothesized effect of *EFF* on *PR* is that *EFF* is fairly stable over time. We have no strong empirical evidence on this point, although none of the previous studies noted in chapter 2 is inconsistent. There is also evidence that production functions fitted to industry data show coefficients that are stable over time (Mairesse and Griliches 1988); that is a necessary condition for the stability of measured technical efficiency but not a sufficient one.

8.3 Statistical Results

To summarize the model, we expect an industry's productivity growth over 1977–1986 (*PR*, real shipments per employee) to increase with its technical efficiency in 1977 (*EFF* or *EFFAJ*), its rate of increase in real shipments (*RQ*), its level of R&D spending relative to sales

($R\&D$), its ratio of gross capital expenditures to employees over 1977–1986 ($\triangle K/L$), and the importance of production scale economies (MES/CDR); it could either increase or decrease with the change in the ratio of imports to domestic supply ($\triangle MS$). The model was estimated for 221 industries (out of the sample used in chapter 6) for which the necessary data were available. Heteroskedasticity-consistent standard errors are reported.

Significance of PR's Determinants

The results are reported in table 8.1, which presents four models needed to deal with issues of robustness that arose. Each model appears in two versions with *EFF* and *EFFAJ* as alternative regressors. We look first at the control variables. The effects of new-capital intensity ($\triangle K/L$) and $R\&D$ are positive as predicted and highly significant. The sole exception is that the inclusion of the rate of growth of real shipments in equations 2a and 2b renders $R\&D$ insignificant. The "Verdoorn's law" variable itself is highly significant; our disinclination to give it a strong causal interpretation was explained. The variable MES/CDR, included as an instrument to capture potential productivity gains due to learning, takes a significant positive coefficient in equations 3a and 3b, but it affects the significance of the measure of technical efficiency.

The variable of central concern, *EFF* (or *EFFAJ*), takes a positive coefficient as predicted, but its significance varies from model to model. With the growth of real shipments controlled (equations 2a and 2b), it is significant at 5 percent (one-tail test). With RQ omitted from the model, its significance level ranges between 6 and 11 percent in all equations except 3a. Recall from chapter 6 that minimum efficient plant scale, one component of MES/CDR, was a significant and strong determinant of technical efficiency. The shaky results of equations 3a and 3b thus indicate that the effects of production scale economies (by learning) and technical efficiency are not entirely disentangled. The purified version *EFFAJ* is not more significant in every model, but its coefficient is larger. The overall conclusion must be that a positive effect of technical efficiency on productivity gains is supported but not at a statistically strong level and/or in clear isolation from other influences.[13]

The effect of the change in import competition remains to be discussed. As with *EFF*, its coefficient is always positive, but its signif-

Table 8.1
Determinants of growth of real output per employee, U.S. manufacturing industries, 1977–1986

	EFF/EFFAJ	ΔK/L	R&D	ΔMS	RQ	MES/CDR	ΔMSL	Constant	$\bar{R}^2$
1a.	0.020	0.001	0.005	0.042				0.003	0.115
	(1.62)	(2.74)	(2.56)	(1.20)				(0.46)	
1b.	0.054	0.002	0.004	0.039				0.007	0.095
	(1.63)	(6.82)	(2.48)	(1.79)				(2.10)	
2a.	0.027	0.001	0.001	0.096	0.004			0.002	0.374
	(2.38)	(3.06)	(0.77)	(2.76)	(6.45)			(0.42)	
2b.	0.057	0.001	0.001	0.094	0.004			0.009	0.364
	(1.93)	(5.78)	(0.66)	(3.39)	(7.50)			(3.38)	
3a.	0.011	0.001	0.004	0.038		0.147		0.004	0.130
	(0.97)	(2.45)	(2.14)	(1.07)		(1.77)		(0.80)	
3b.	0.041	0.001	0.003	0.013		0.199		0.007	0.122
	(1.37)	(5.73)	(1.98)	(0.71)		(2.74)		(2.09)	
4a.	0.018	0.001	0.005	0.035			0.068	0.002	0.119
	(1.45)	(2.79)	(2.64)	(0.94)			(1.15)	(0.42)	
4b.	0.044	0.002	0.004	0.044			0.210	0.004	0.146
	(1.26)	(3.42)	(2.62)	(1.96)			(4.76)	(1.15)	

icance level depends on the specification. It is highly significant (1 percent, two-tail test) if RQ is included in the model (equation 2) but otherwise does not rise above 10 percent (two-tail test).[14] We wondered about the time structure of the influence of $\triangle MS$'s influence on PR because any hypothesis about the effect of unanticipated changes in the supply of competing imports implies a protracted adjustment subject to some distributed lag. As a first-cut exploration, we added to the model (equation 4) the change in imports' share between 1972 and 1977, denoted $\triangle MSL$. In equation 4b its coefficient is highly significant, and in both 4a and 4b the coefficient's magnitude exceeds that for $\triangle MS$.[15] Conclusions cannot be stated with great confidence in the face of fluctuating significance levels, but the data evidently do not reject the hypothesis that increasing import competition elevates the productivity growth rate of competing domestic producers, with the effect subject to substantial lags because of its dependence on discrete investment and divestment decisions.

Supplemental Evidence

Several supplemental conclusions from the data help us to assess and interpret these results. First, recall that EFF cannot be calculated from the stochastic frontier production estimated for every industry. The missing cases are typically those in which the residuals around the fitted production are skewed in the wrong direction. A possible interpretation is that these industries have no appreciable technical efficiency, and some, although not all, of the evidence cited in chapters 4 and 6 is consistent with this interpretation. If it holds for the relation just estimated, PR should be higher for industries with EFF missing than for industries for which EFF could be calculated. The mean value of PR for the former group is indeed 5 percent higher, but the difference is not statistically significant.

Several correlations in the data underlying the regression model are revealing. PR, estimated for 1977–1986, is only moderately correlated with its counterpart estimated for 1972–1977 period, 0.20. While this value is highly significant statistically, it leaves ample room for PR to be affected by changes that occurred during 1977–1986, as the regression model indicates. A plot of values of PR for 1972–1977 and 1977–1986 reveals a modest number of industries that exhibit high productivity gains in both 1972–1977 and 1977–1986, while the relation appears largely random for the majority of industries with low productivity gains. It is plausible that the leverage of both import competition and technical efficiency is exerted mainly on industries with modest technological opportunities for productivity growth.[16]

If an industry's efficiency enhances its subsequent productivity growth, one wonders exactly what productivity-raising reallocations are involved. Correlations were examined between *EFF* and several measures of changes in industries' use of resources, taken from the *U.S. Industrial Outlook* data base. We found a negative correlation (−0.135, significant at 2 percent) between *EFF* and the 1977–1986 change in industries' payroll-shipments ratios. *EFF* is uncorrelated with changes in average hourly wage rates, so the gain was in reduced labor usage, not compensation.[17] Reduced labor usage obviously had to be accompanied with increased usage of other inputs. *EFF*'s correlation with the change in materials/shipments is positive although not significant. More efficient labor use was apparently not attained chiefly through substituting capital for labor; the correlation between *EFF* and $\triangle K/L$ is in fact negative and highly significant, −0.312.

The effect of $\triangle MS$ on *PR* was probed in several ways. Here the smaller BLS sample proved useful because its data could be extended back to the 1960s (the main ITA data base begins in 1972). We gathered data on imports' shares of domestic supply (imports plus production) and also shares of domestic production exported for the eighty-eight BLS industries in 1967, 1977, and 1982,[18] and obtained labor productivity growth rates for 1967–1977 and 1977–1984. The level of import penetration in 1967 was uncorrelated with subsequent productivity growth; the correlation is negative for 1967–1977 and positive for 1977–1984 but significant in neither.

Now consider the correlations between productivity growth and changes in trade exposure—the relationship found positive and (erratically) significant in the regression model based on ITA data. The change in import penetration[19] is also positively correlated with productivity growth after 1977 (0.15) in the BLS sample but negatively correlated with productivity growth before 1977 (−0.22, significant at 5 percent). This contrast is interesting in relation to the effect of $\triangle MSL$ in table 8.1, equation 4. We note one more relationship: the correlation between the change in import shares (1967–1982) and the change in productivity growth from 1967–1977 to 1977–1984. This is 0.33, significant at 1 percent and rather stronger than the correlations between trade-share changes and the productivity growth rates themselves.

Taking together these correlations observed in the BLS sample, we can tentatively conclude that the relation between PR and the change in import penetration found in the ITA data for 1977–1986 does not extend back to the 1967–1977 period. Nonetheless, the correlations just reported are consistent with a cumulative effect of import competition over the longer period from 1967 to the mid-1980s. They are also consistent with the strong (though not precisely estimated) effect of import penetration in 1972–1977 on productivity growth in 1977–1986, shown in table 8.1.[20] No hypothesis suggests why a bend in productivity growth rates due to intensifying import competition should center on 1977. That year was picked fortuitously as the year of our efficiency measures and was not screened inductively.

Correlations in the data also help to bring exports into the picture and test a corollary of the findings of table 8.1. If increased import competition bestirs productivity growth, which in turn improves the industry's comparative-advantage position, we have the odd-sounding implication that extra imports beget extra exports. Yet that relation is exactly consistent with the widely observed growth of intraindustry trade among the industrial countries since World War II. It is also consistent with correlations in the data base. Neoclassical theory of international trade predicts that an industry with import competition will have no exports; if it nonetheless does, changes in imports' share of supply should be negatively correlated with changes in the shares of output exported. Intraindustry trade implies that they will be positively correlated. The correlations are indeed positive if not very high: 0.124 for 1977–1986, significant at 7 percent, and 0.103 for 1972–1977.[21] The consistency of our main findings with the literature on intraindustry trade increases the credibility of the main findings of table 8.1, but it also raises some issues about long-run intersectoral allocations.

8.4 Summary and Conclusions

Because the preceding chapters have validated the measurement of technical efficiency, in the sense of failing to reject many hypotheses about its determinants, it seemed desirable to investigate some of its effects as well. One possible effect is on the industry's rate of productivity growth (relative to its potential). If an industry's technical efficiency is fairly stable over time (as seems likely, although not tested directly in this study), static efficiency could exert a positive effect on dynamic efficiency—productivity growth. The hypothesis rests on a simple and primitive proposition: that business units unsuccessful at matching current best-practice productivity are unlikely to perform well in improving productivity. While that proposition cannot be given a strong neoclassical basis, it accords well with many ideas found in the literature on organizational and behavioral approaches to the firm. Furthermore, while some problems of aggegation arise, in general the hypothesis that inefficiency retards productivity growth translates from the individual business unit to the industry.

To test the effect of technical efficiency on productivity growth, we related the growth of real shipments per employee over 1977–1986 to technical efficiency in 1977. Several variables were employed to control for productivity-growth opportunities: research and development activity, gross fixed investment per employee over the period, extent of production scale economies (apparently an important determinant of proprietary learning), and the rate of output (demand?) growth. Each of these exerts a significant positive influence. With them controlled, technical efficiency wields an influence that is always positive and generally significant at 10 percent, but its significance is somewhat sensitive to the specification of the model. When we remove spurious components from the measure of technical efficiency, the magnitude of its coefficient rises, but its significance increases only in some specifications.

The same qualified acceptance was accorded to another behavioral hypothesis: that productivity growth is affected by changes in the intensity of import competition. Most, although not all, theoretical considerations suggest that the increased import competition faced by the typical U.S. manufacturing industry in the past two decades should increase domestic competitors' productivity. The empirical relation is uniformly positive, although its significance is somewhat sensitive to specification. It seems to operate with a substantial lag, although the cross-section model was not designed to identify the time structure accurately.

The relation of technical efficiency to productivity growth has important long-term implications that we have so far ignored. Assume that the output of U.S. producers is an imperfect substitute for the outputs of their overseas competitors but that U.S. output is small relative to the world market. That is, the U.S. producers comprise one segment of an industry that is monopolistically competitive world-wide. The lower is the technical efficiency of the U.S. industry, the less favorable is the price-attribute mix that its typical producer can offer on the world market; given the technical efficiency of producers elsewhere, the smaller should the U.S. industry be in the long run. That is, the technical efficiency that its producers can attain joins with the traditional determinants of comparative advantage as well as the technical-efficiency levels of other U.S. industries to determine its ability to recruit and retain part of the U.S. stock of factors of production.

Now consider the relation between technical efficiency and productivity growth. We assume that the potential for productivity growth of each worldwide industry may be realized in varying degrees by its different national branches. Assume also the empirical result supported in this chapter: that technical inefficiency drags down an industry's actual relative to its potential rate of productivity growth. Then, with general equilibrium factors held constant, the industry falls into a vicious (or virtuous) circle: low (high) efficiency means low (high) productivity growth and further deterioration (improvement) of the industry's international competitiveness and contraction (enlargement) of its size.

But another dynamic linkage must be considered: the positive effect on productivity growth of increasing import competition, tentatively supported in our empirical analysis. Suppose that import competition increases because foreign producers have developed improved varieties or raised their productivity faster than their domestic rivals. Imports' share of the domestic market tends to expand, inducing (on our evidence) productivity improvement by the domestic producers. Unless this improvement results solely from removal of the least efficient inputs from the domestic industry, it tends to limit the displacement and contraction of domestic producers, attenuating the vicious (or virtuous) cycle.

These long-run relations have several implications. First, they indicate that our simple test of the relation between efficiency and productivity growth is taken in a parochial context. It should be viewed as exposing part of (what appears to be) a set of interacting long-term relationships that determine the positions of particular national industries and indeed the general equilibrium structure of production and trade.

Second, they affect the long-term stability of technical efficiency—a question we could not address empirically (due to resource constraints) and one that has received little attention anywhere. Import competition has favorable effects on both productivity growth (shown in this chapter) and on technical efficiency itself (shown in chapter 6). Technical efficiency must therefore change over time. Indeed we conjecture that part of the productivity gains responding to increased import competition represent the reduction of technical inefficiency.

Third, they raise a number of interesting questions for future research, especially research that entails the measurement of technical efficiency at different points in time. Technical efficiency appears to be endogenous in a system of long-run relationships. While its interdependence with productivity growth and international competition are the endogenizing forces highlighted here, other changes should also affect technical efficiency, productivity growth, and the industry's scale of operation. Technological changes affecting minimum efficient plant scale is one obvious example. Another is changes in economic organization such as in the extent of corporate diversification. The current wave of leveraged buy outs and the apparent rectification of inefficient diversification through interfirm trade in business units may affect technical efficiency and thus industries' productivity growth rates and international competitive positions. Admittedly, as research subjects these relationships have the undesirable property that they proceed at a slow pace, making inferential leverage hard to obtain. They raise the payout to close-in study of the adjustment process, as an alternative to comparisons of before and after positions that are far separated in time.

9   Conclusions and Implications

To conclude this study, we offer thoughts on two subjects—implications of our findings for policy and possible lines of future research.

9.1 Policy Implications

Although we could not draw confident conclusions about the power of competition among domestic sellers to promote efficiency, the results are consistent in many ways with that hypothesis. First, we judge that maximum levels of technical efficiency are found in U.S. industries with producer concentration below the level at which oligopolistic behavior sets in (although not "very low").[1] While the findings about domestic competition are qualified, import competition has clearly been favorable to technical efficiency. Not only does it exert a significant positive influence on static efficiency (chapter 6), but also changes (not levels) of import rivalry may have increased industries' rates of productivity growth (chapter 8; this relationship is not entirely robust statistically).

Overall this study's findings support public policy to enforce competition among domestic producers and counsel resisting the temptation to shelter them from pressures by foreign rivals. Statistical evidence in the field of industrial organization has failed to reject the hypotheses that collusive behavior (price fixing, for example) aids the survival of inefficient units and shifts rivalry toward other forms that tempt some rivals to make socially excessive levels of certain types of outlays. Our evidence agrees with those results and supports inducing firms to compete openly in their pricing. The negative consequences of protection from imports are equally clear, especially protection taking the form most evident—abundant, if allegedly temporary, relief for producer groups facing stepped-up rivalry from abroad. Also negative are this study's implications for some stylish new models of industrial policy, which call for the government to cosset the national member of an international oligopoly in the hope that this fortified enterprise will then divert rents accruing to the international oligopoly into the national income and away from foreign pockets.

Many people believe intuitively that efficiency is hard to attain in complex organizations where rent-seeking activities can flourish, individuals can appropriate benefits in the form of costly commitments of policies and resources, and the revision of an inefficient set of implicit commitments is a costly and uncertain process for a chief executive or other intervenor. In activities that must be carried on by such complex organizations, tolerable levels of efficiency can be sustained only if outside organizations—rivals or enemies—pose a significantly strong threat to the organization that the opportunism of its members can be kept at bay.

Although our study does not test that view directly, none of our results is inconsistent with it. We found, most notably, that enterprise diversification is hostile to an industry's efficiency; while our research design is not set up to target the individual firm, it goes some of the distance in showing that the size class of establishments with the greater inefficiency is the one in which parents are most likely to be diversified (chapter 7). Other evidence from industrial organization shows that reduced efficiency is the consequence of operating diversified businesses acquired in corporate mergers.

The policy conclusions from that finding seem obvious but must be stated with some care. First, some diversification is evidently effective for achieving synergies, as we know from studies of the determinants of interindustry patterns of diversification (Lemelin 1982; MacDonald 1985). Second, avoiding excess diversification by the method currently most popular—protecting potential target firms from takeovers—probably just trades one form of inefficiency (suboptimal use of resources managed by the targets) for another (suboptimal deployment of diversified resources by managers inexperienced in their supervision). Furthermore, traditional policy proposals to limit growth or acquisitions by absolutely large firms are not close to the mark because the problem identified in this study is apparently not one of absolute size per se.[2] The best prescription consistent with our findings seems to be encouragements by taxation and other means for managers of large and mature enterprises to return cash flows to their shareholders rather than squander them on conglomerate mergers or other low-value uses.[3]

An optimist reviewing our strictures about diversification might hold that the flogged nag is already moribund. The market for corporate divisions now transfers many business units from firms less able to manage them to enterprises where a better fit is afforded. Management buy outs have been shown to create real value (as well as tax benefits) by focusing the incentives of the now-controlling managers and averting many of the principal-agent problems that harass the large, multibusiness firm. While the state of U.S. corporate organization seems improved since 1977, acquisition fever is hardly extinct in large U.S. enterprises, and this reverse form of Asian flu is making inroads among foreign (would-be) multinational firms and European companies contemplating the changes scheduled for 1992 in the European Community.

Another policy issue is flagged by our finding that technical efficiency is negatively related to the presence of trade unions in industries that operate large plants. Because policy toward industrial relations is both distant from our competence and much fought over by others, our remarks here are tentative. That trade unions might impair efficiency through work rules, jurisdictional restrictions, and other forms of policy rent seeking seems plausible enough. It is consistent with the evidence that unions appear and take pecuniary rents where those rents are available (as potential monopoly profits). And it is not in conflict with the proposition (Freeman and Medoff 1984) that unions can increase efficiency by improving communications and agency relations. The relative weight of these effects evidently depends on the structure of the industry, and it would require an investigation more focused than this one to isolate them and establish their relative force.

The nominally positive findings of this study indicate the structural influences that do and do not contribute importantly to explaining differences in apparent efficiency among plants and firms. That information itself has normative value—as information for business managers about what decisions may matter the most and as background for policymakers concerned with how much leverage particular policies can exert. Take, for example, our finding, in accord with other research on technical efficiency (Førsund and Hjalmarsson 1987), that capital-vintage distributions are an important source of dispersion in units' efficiency levels. The finding does not imply that too little replacement investment takes place. For business managers, however, it suggests the importance of devoting managerial resources to make sure that replacement and modernization decisions are optimized. And for policymakers it indicates that investment incentives are likely to have substantial effects (good or bad) on vintage distributions.

9.2 Further Research

We undertook this project with much uncertainty about its prospective value. It required a large commitment of resources, and previous empirical research supplied little guidance for anticipating whether the results would bring a commensurate reward. We feel that the payout ex post meets the test of opportunity cost and warrants consideration of further research along this line.

A natural sequel to this study is application of its approach to other industrial countries. The conclusions we reached are properly tested by replication on other economies. Previous transnational research on industrial organization suffices to establish that the effects of market structures on competitive processes and resource allocations are not very sensitive to the observed differences in cultures and legal systems among the industrial countries. On the other hand, such differences may lend themselves to comparative test, if specific hypotheses can be formed about how a country's distinctive institution should affect the efficiency of its manufacturing industries. For example, Japanese industries may show residual effects of factor-price distortions (now waning) such that wage rates increased and capital costs decreased with the sizes of enterprises, just as British industries might show the effects of the United Kingdom's legacy of particularly exacerbated labor relations.[4]

Similar studies for other industrial countries hold promise running considerably beyond the replication of the findings at hand. Consider the average levels of productivity exhibited in two countries' national branches of some given manufacturing industry. They will differ in average efficiency because (1) one country may enjoy a superior efficiency frontier due to proprietary technology, undiffused innovations of other types, country-specific superiorities of effort, organization, policy, and the like, and (2) the two national branches may differ in the degree to which their producers' actual efficiency levels fall short of the respective national frontiers. With data available on both average productivity differences and on levels of technical efficiency in each industry, it becomes possible to infer the relative positions of the unobserved national frontiers and to test hypotheses about the roles of factors governing the placement and adjustment of these national frontiers.

Another line of research suggested by our findings is the persistence of technical efficiency over time. No broadly based evidence exists on the stability of industries' efficiency levels over time. Yet chapter 8 presented tantalizing, if inconclusive, evidence on the issues of the dynamics. Do extreme levels of technical (in)efficiency tend to reverse themselves, and if so at what rate? Do major disturbances (an energy shock, an unanticipated major change in import competition) affect technical efficiency and (if so) through interaction with what other traits of market structure? How are changes in technical efficiency and changes in an industry's overall size related (that is, how does technical efficiency relate to the subtraction of resources from the industry, or their addition)? Do industries experience persistent trends in their levels of efficiency, and (if so) what forces drive them?

Fortunately, the use of panel data in industrial economics is expanding rapidly and with it access to data bases on plants and firms that may prove suitable for answering these questions. An obvious line of extension is to measure technical-efficiency levels of industries at different points in time. This procedure would support a more satisfying approach to the dynamic issues than the method used in chapter 8 by allowing a cleaner partition of changes in industries' productivity levels into changes in the frontiers and changes in the dispersion of producers below the current frontier. Furthermore, access to panel data on individual plants would make feasible the tracing of technical-efficiency changes to particular units and relating those changes to these units' situations and opportunities.

Appendix

Sources of Exogenous Variables

In this appendix we provide a glossary of the exogenous variables used in the analysis and report their sources and any particular features of their construction. Most data were organized by means of the PICA data base, Division of Research, Graduate School of Business Administration, Harvard University. This data base contains many variables available on the four-digit Standard Industrial Classification or other conformable classification systems; PICA data were originally obtained in machine-readable form whenever possible. When a variable is available only for an industry category more aggregated than the four-digit SIC, we assume that ratios for the aggregate industry pertain to each four-digit SIC it contains and that total magnitudes are distributed among them in the same way as total shipments. Most exogenous variables should exhibit little year-to-year variation. The year 1977 was employed whenever possible, but we utilized earlier years in some cases. Variables are listed in alphabetical order according to the notation introduced in chapters 5 through 8.

ADS
: Ratio of purchased advertising services to industry shipments, 1972. Source: Bureau of Economic Analysis, Department of Commerce, data tape of Input-Output Tables. When our data base was organized, 1972 was the latest year available.

C4AJ
: Fraction of shipments accounted for by the four largest firms, 1977, adjusted for international competition, interindustry competition, overaggregation and non-competing subproducts, and geographically fragmented markets. Source: Leonard W. Weiss and George A. Pascoe, *Adjusted Concentration Ratios in Manufacturing, 1972 and 1977* (Washington, D.C.: Federal Trade Commission, 1986).

CDR   Output per employee in plants smaller than (approx-
             imately) the unit accounting for the fiftieth percentile
             of industry output, divided by output per employee in
             plants larger than this value, 1977 (a rough proxy for
             the extent of scale economies). Source: Calculated from
             U.S. Bureau of the Census, *1977 Census of Manufactures*
             tape.

CONC   Percentage of shipments accounted for by the four
             largest firms, 1977. Source: Bureau of the Census, *1977
             Census of Manufactures, Special Report Series, Concentra-
             tion Ratios in Manufacturing*, MC77(SR-9).

COSIZE   Average size of the four largest companies, estimated
             by multiplying total industry shipments by the average
             fraction of shipments accounted for by the largest four
             companies (see *CONC*). Source: Bureau of the Census,
             1977 Census of Manufactures data tape; also see *CONC*.

COVE   Ratio of sales by establishments belonging to enter-
             prises classified to other industries to sales by all estab-
             lishments classified to this industry, 1972. Source:
             Bureau of the Census, *Enterprise Statistics, 1972. Part I:
             General Report on Industrial Organization*; later enterprise
             statistics had not been released when the data base was
             prepared.

DIST   Mean distance over which industry tonnage was ship-
             ped, 1977. Source: Bureau of the Census, *Census of
             Transportation, 1977*.

DIV   Sum of *COVE* and *SPECE*.

FUEL   Cost of purchased fuels and energy divided by pur-
             chased inputs, unweighted average of plants included
             in the Annual Survey of Manufactures. Source: Bureau
             of the Census (calculated during the estimation of the
             frontier production functions).

FUELVAR   Standard deviation of ratio of purchased fuels and
             energy to total purchased inputs, plants included in
             Annual Survey of Manufactures panel, 1977, multi-
             plied (weighted) by *FUEL*. Source: Bureau of the Cen-
             sus (calculated during the estimation of the frontier
             production functions).

GROW   Proportional rate of growth of real output, 1968–1977.
              Source: Bureau of Labor Statistics, *Time Series Data for
              Input-Output Industries*, bulletin no. 2018 (1979).

$\triangle K/L$ Sum of (undeflated) annual gross capital expenditures
              by the industry, 1977–1986, divided by sum of annual
              average employment levels. Source: *U.S. Industrial
              Outlook* data base (originally Bureau of the Census).

KSIZE   Estimated capital required to construct the industry's
              median-sized plant, 1977. Estimated employment in
              the median-sized plant (see *PSIZE*) was multiplied by
              the industry's average ratio of total assets to employ-
              ment. Source (total assets): Bureau of the Census,
              Annual Survey of Manufactures, 1976.

MAD   Expenditures on media advertising as a proportion of
              total sales, 1974–1976. Source: Federal Trade Commis-
              sion, *Statistical Report: Annual Line of Business Report*.
              We mainly relied on 1976 annual data but inserted
              values for 1974 or 1975 for industries missing in 1976.

MEAN(K/L)   Unweighted mean ratio of adjusted capital to adjusted
              labor, plants included in the Annual Survey of Manu-
              factures panel, 1977. Source: Bureau of the Census
              (calculated during the estimation of frontier production
              functions).

MES/CDR   *RSIZE* divided by *CDR*.

MS   Imports divided by industry shipments plus imports,
              averaged over 1972–1976. Source: *U.S. Industrial Out-
              look* data base, Department of Commerce. This data
              base results from an extensive effort to match the
              commodity-based international trade classification
              (TSUSA) to the industry-based classification (SIC) used
              for production statistics.

$\triangle MS$ Ratio of imports to the sum of imports and shipments
              of competing domestic products, 1986, minus the cor-
              responding ratio for 1977. Source: *U.S. Industrial Out-
              look* data base (data originally from Bureau of the
              Census).

MULT   Sales by establishments belonging to companies that
              are multiplant operators in this industry, divided by

sales of all establishments classified to the industry, 1972. Source: see *COVE*.

NOBS   Square root of the number of plants contained in the Annual Survey of Manufactures panel, 1977, and utilized in estimation of frontier production functions. Source: Bureau of the Census (calculated during estimation of frontier production functions).

NPWVAR   Standard deviation of ratio of nonproduction workers to total employees, plants included in the Annual Survey of Manufactures panel, 1977, multiplied by the industry's overall ratio of nonproduction workers to total employees. Source: Bureau of the Census data (calculated during the estimation of frontier production functions).

PART   Proportion of part-time workers, estimated from the number of hours worked per employee in 1977, on the assumption that full-time employees work 2,000 hours a year, part-time employees 1,000 hours. Source: Bureau of the Census, *1977 Census of Manufactures* tape.

PC1   Principal component that indicates positively the unimportance of the product's individual purchases to the buyer ("convenience good") and its affinity for information-based product differentiation; negatively, the component indicates intrinsic complexity and heterogeneity of the product. This and other components were extracted from underlying series indicating company-financed R&D as a proportion of sales, media advertising as a proportion of sales, degree to which production is to order, infrequency of purchase, importance of auxiliary services to the buyer, importance of purchase to the buyer, and degree to which selection is made by a specifier (agent other than the user). *PC1* is the rotated first principal component from these variables. Sources: Federal Trade Commission, *Statistical Report: Annual Line of Business Report, 1976*; Earl F. Bailey, *Marketing-Cost Ratios of U.S. Manufacturers: A Technical Analysis* (New York: Conference Board, 1975).

PC2   Principal component (second component following *PC1*) that indicates positively the intersection between heterogeneity and information as bases for product differentiation—innovative goods subject to extensive information flows and auxiliary services provided by sellers to buyers. For sources and construction, see *PC1*.

PC3   Principal component (third component following *PC1* and *PC2*) that positively indicates that sales promotion efforts are oriented toward distribution channels or specifiers rather than ultimate buyers. For sources and construction, see *PC1*.

PR   Annualized rate of growth of real shipments per employee, 1977–1986. Source: *U.S. Industrial Outlook* data base.

PROD   Proportional growth rate of labor productivity (real output per employee-hour), 1968–1977. Source: Bureau of Labor Statistics, data tape corresponding to the publication *Time Series Data for Input-Output Industries*, bulletin no. 2018 (1979). Most observations pertain to three-digit SIC industries.

PSIZE   Approximate size of the plant accounting for the median unit of industry shipments, 1977. This variable is estimated as shipments of plants in the employment size class containing median shipments, divided by the number of plants in this class. Source: Bureau of the Census, *1977 Census of Manufactures* data tape.

R&D   Company-financed research and development spending as a proportion of total sales, 1974–1976. Source: Federal Trade Commission, *Statistical Report: Annual Line of Business Report*. We mainly relied on 1976 annual data but inserted values for 1974 or 1975 for industries missing in 1976. If no data were available, we plugged in the corresponding ratio taken from National Science Foundation, *Research and Development in Industry*.

RAD   Radius (miles) within which 80 percent of the industry's tonnage was shipped, 1977. Source: Bureau of the Census, *Census of Transportation, 1977*.

RAW   Sum of the industry's input coefficients from primary sectors (agriculture, forestry, fishing, mining), 1972.

	Source: Bureau of Economic Analysis, Department of Commerce, data tape of Input-Output Tables, 1972. When our data base was organized, 1972 was the most recent year available.
RQ	Annualized rate of growth of deflated shipments, 1977–1986. *Source*: *U.S. Industrial Outlook* data base.
RSIZE	Approximate size (shipments) of the plant accounting for the median unit of industry shipments (see *PSIZE*), divided by total industry shipments, 1977. Source: Bureau of the Census, *1977 Census of Manufactures* tape.
SD(DK/K)	Standard deviation of ratios of gross capital expenditure to value of capital stock, plants included in Annual Survey of Manufactures panel, 1977. Source: Bureau of the Census (calculated during estimation of frontier production functions).
SD(K/L)	Standard deviation of ratio of adjusted capital stock to adjusted labor input, plants included in the Annual Survey of Manufactures panel, 1977. The adjustments are described in section 3.2. Source: Bureau of the Census (calculated during the estimation of the frontier production functions).
SD(MACH/K)	Standard deviation of ratio of machinery to total capital, plants included in the Annual Survey of Manufactures panel, 1977. Source: Bureau of the Census (calculated during estimation of frontier production functions).
SD(WAGE)	Standard deviation of total payroll per production worker hour, plants included in the Annual Survey of Manufactures panel, 1977. Source: Bureau of the Census (calculated during the estimation of frontier production functions).
SPECE	Ratio of value of shipments by plants classified to other industries but controlled by enterprises classified to be industry at hand, to shipments by all plants controlled by firms classified to the industry, 1972. Source: See *COVE*.

SPECP   One minus industry specialization ratio (shipments of
             products classified to the industry by plants classified
             to the industry, divided by total shipments of those
             plants), 1977. Source: Bureau of the Census, *1977 Census of Manufactures* tape.

UNION   Proportion of production workers who were union
             members, early 1970s. Source: Richard B. Freeman and
             James L. Medoff, "New Estimates of Private Sector
             Unionism in the United States," *Industrial and Labor
             Relations Review* 32 (January 1979), 143–74.

VINTM   Percentage of gross equipment less than five years old
             plus percentage more than twenty years old, 1976.
             Source: Office of Economic Growth, Bureau of Labor
             Statistics, machine-readable data base described in
             Capital Stocks Estimates for Input-Output Industries:
             Methods and Data, bulletin no. 2034 (1979).

VINTP   Percentage of gross plant less than five years old plus
             percentage more than thirty years old, 1976. Source:
             see *VINTM*.

VIOL   Number of indictments for violations of Sherman Act
             Section 1 brought against firms classified to the indus-
             try, 1958–1977. Source: James M. Clabault and Michael
             K. Block, *Sherman Act Indictments, 1955–1980* (New
             York: Federal Legal Publications, 1981).

XS   Exports divided by industry shipments, 1972–1976. For
             source and description, see *MS*.

Notes

Introduction

1. He noted the difference in capital intensity between factories (using power) and workshops (without), as well as the range in workshop figures associated with specialist activities. He also highlighted regional differences and differences due to hours of utilization in the day and fluctuations in "normal employment" over seasons of the year.

2. Frantz (1988) surveyed the subsequent controversy over the meaning and extent of X-inefficiency.

3. Some hypotheses naturally address themselves to the efficiency levels of differently situated firms within a given industry. Examples of this empirical approach are mentioned in chapter 2.

4. Apart from these points of principle, we could feasibly obtain measures of technical efficiency only for a single year, and Census disclosure rules block any approach that exposes the identities of particular (efficient or inefficient) plants or firms. Thus the best choice was in fact the only one.

5. The average is sensitive to the specification of the production function and the way in which technical efficiency is expressed.

Chapter 2

1. Later writers also apply the term "allocative inefficiency" to what Farrell called price inefficiency because it does indeed represent general allocative inefficiency due to input choices by the enterprise.

2. Because of the familiar duality relationships between production functions and cost functions, these inefficiency measures can, under certain assumptions, be stated equivalently as excess input costs per unit of output or as discrepancies between actual output and the potential maximum output obtained from a given bundle of inputs. Later writers (Førsund and Hjalmarsson 1974; Kopp 1981) pointed out that with nonconstant returns to scale, the

estimated extent of technical inefficiency differs depending on whether an excess-input or a deficient-output measure is used. However, neither measure is intrinsically superior to the other.

3. The following survey will be brief and nontechnical. For fuller accounts see Førsund, Lovell, and Schmidt (1980), Kopp (1981), and Schmidt (1985–1986). We can also note an independent approach to efficiency measurement proposed by Downie (1958), who focused on the variation of profit rates of competing firms.

4. Some researchers have gotten around this difficulty by the sensible if ad hoc expedient of discarding a few observations of the apparently most efficient units and reestimating the production frontier, to test for the stability of the estimated parameters of the production function. See Meller (1976).

5. Estimation by corrected ordinary least squares is asymptotically less efficient than by maximum likelihood, but Olson, Schmidt, and Waldman (1980) reported a Monte Carlo study showing that the former technique generally performs as well as the latter for the case of the half-normal u distribution, and it is simpler to estimate. However, compare Greene's (1980b) empirical results.

6. However, Akio Torii has shown (in an unpublished communication) that inefficiency following the half-normal distribution can be predicted if units' cost levels have a natural tendency to slip upward at a constant rate per unit of time, but managers act decisively to knock the inefficiency back down to a zero level with a probability that increases with the (cumulative) level of inefficiency.

7. It is known that the gamma distribution employed by Richmond (1974) gives quite different average results; see Førsund, Lovell, and Schmidt (1980, p. 13).

8. Schmidt and Lovell (1980) did find that technical and price inefficiency are positively correlated for a sample of steam-electric generating plants. There does not seem to have been any research on the implications for the measurement and analysis of technical inefficiency of neglecting the occurrence of inappropriate input choices (price inefficiency).

9. Meller's procedure is somewhat vulnerable to errors in the data that could permit the efficiency frontiers to be strongly affected by erroneous observations. Data errors that are proportionally larger for small than for large firms could account for his relationship between size and technical efficiency.

10. Pitt and Lee (1981) and Chen and Tang (1987) found that individual firms' efficiency levels decreased significantly with their ages. Førsund and Hjalmarsson (1987) extensively investigated vintage effects in several Scandinavian manufacturing industries. Also of interest is Summa's (1985) study of the Finnish brewing industry, in which an analysis of vintage effects and technical progress is interwoven with the industry's absorption of a major change in public policy.

11. The slope coefficients of the frontier production function differ from those of a conventional statistical production function fitted by ordinary least squares only when linear programming techniques or statistical maximum-likelihood methods are used to estimate the frontier function. Otherwise the frontier function differs only by an intercept shift that indicates the average extent of technical inefficiency. Another procedure used in some linear-programming models of the frontier is to compare characteristics of the firms determined to be on or near the frontier with those of the remaining units.

12. Meller (1976) suggested some explanations for the apparently high levels of technical inefficiency that he found in Chilean manufacturing industries, but he did not formally test them in cross-section. He did find that efficient plants pay relatively high wages, which could indicate either an affinity of skill for efficiency or a transfer to the work force of the efficiency rents flowing to the better plants.

13. The point is also made that the Cobb-Douglas and CES have the property of self-duality, meaning that both the production and cost functions are members of the same family of functional forms. Translog does not have this property (Burgess 1975). However, inadequacies of the data in any case make it impossible to deal with cost functions in this study, and so the matter is not one of practical concern.

14. The increase is statistically significant for more than one-third of the industries and insignificant in the rest of those industries showing increases. The test was performed by regressing the ratio of depreciable assets to sales on asset size for the various asset-size classes of firms reported by the Internal Revenue Service and then examining the significance of the resulting slope coefficients.

15. An exception is Shen (1965), who estimated expansion paths for two-digit manufacturing industries and found without exception a tendency for the larger plants to be more capital intensive.

16. We have so far taken for granted that sufficient substitutability exists among inputs in most manufacturing processes to rule out the use of a fixed-coefficients (or Leontief) form. Rather high degrees of substitutability are found in a number of studies, such as those appearing in Berndt and Field (1981).

17. These also require a production function sufficiently tractable to allow derivation of the cost and input demand frontiers in closed form. See Førsund, Lovell, and Schmidt (1980, pp. 15–16).

18. One of the better arguments for excluding materials inputs from the analysis is that their quantities can normally be adjusted to realized changes in output within the course of a year (our period of observation), whereas capital and labor inputs are more nearly exogenous.

Chapter 3

1. When the methodology is applied to industries in developing countries, the assumption might seem rather more suspect. As an extension of the present project, we hope to combine analyses of the determinants of international differences in matched industries (e.g., Davies and Caves 1987) and of discrepancies within countries between average and national best-practice productivity, on the presumption that average productivity in two national branches of an industry can be considered the joint result of technical-inefficiency gaps from their own frontiers and differences in those frontiers.

2. Like so many other economic researchers, our procedure will make the final sample one with only a dubious claim to randomness. The option of sampling randomly among four-digit manufacturing industries was declined because of the large number of hypotheses we expected to test and the expectation that missing data would make large inroads on our degrees of freedom.

3. We shall use the terms *enterprise, company,* and *firm* interchangeably to indicate independent business decision-making units that are not subsidiaries of other firms. We use *establishment* and *plant* interchangeably to refer to the Census definition of physical production facilities operating at a single address.

4. We noted in chapter 2 the current interest in estimating frontier production functions on panel data (Schmidt 1985–1986). That desirable step lies beyond the scope of this project.

5. This problem is discussed further in chapter 4.

6. The high correlation between materials input and output is the source of much of this difficulty. For example, we compared the correlations between gross output and capital input with the correlations between gross output and the cross-product of capital and materials inputs (that appears in the translog function). For all twelve industries, the latter correlation exceeds the former. Another factor weighing against gross output is reduced degrees of freedom.

7. The Bureau of the Census uses imputations to cover missing values, consistent with its objective of securing accurate aggregate statistics. Because the imputations are presumably average ratios of some sort, it seems unlikely that this process creates any outliers that affect our stochastic frontier production functions, although it is conceivable that they might extinguish a few outliers.

8. It would be a matter of concern if the editing rules we employed follow on the heels of independent efforts by the Bureau of the Census to impose consistency and plausibility. We understand that the Census's own editing checks are performed on aggregates of establishments (for example, size classes within an industry) rather than on individual establishments' survey re-

sponses. Errors caught by such a procedure should generally be much more gross than those putatively identified by our own editing rules.

9. Data on the numbers of observations rejected on each data rule were not supplied by the Census Bureau for industries in which the total numbers of establishment records rejected were small. Hence the 376 industries for which rejections can be analyzed are the ones more seriously affected. Enough usable establishment records were available to estimate frontier production functions for 434 industries.

Chapter 4

1. Meeusen and van den Broeck (1977a) used a comparable procedure with the one-sided errors assumed to follow the exponential distribution.

2. The following analysis is based on a memorandum prepared by Masu Uekusa and Akio Torii for a parallel project undertaken in Japan.

3. Skewness could be calculated for every industry with enough establishments that the production function could be estimated. However, we include it here only for those industries for which at least one of the other measures could also be estimated.

4. For reasons mentioned previously, the range for $MMGO$ is much smaller than for $MMVA$, although it is still substantial. The mean value of $MMGO$ is 15.2 for NA industries and 20.0 for TI industries; for $MMVA$ these figures are 22.9 and 152.7, respectively.

5. Data on industry and product shipments were in fact available to us for each industry in each year from 1972 to 1985. We tested whether the variability of the mismatch over time was related to the variables in our analysis. For each industry we calculated the maximum and minimum annual values of industry shipments/product shipments over 1972–1985 and subtracted the minimum from the maximum. The mean value of this difference is a bit higher for NA industries (0.25) than for TI industries (0.21); although the difference between means is not significant, the direction agrees with the conclusion stated in the text. Similarly the measure of the variability of the mismatch is uncorrelated with our measures of technical efficiency except for a positive correlation with EFF taken from production functions that use gross output as the dependent variable. Again the absence of negative correlations confirms that we are not inferring technical inefficiency from rough-edged industry definitions.

6. This null hypothesis will reemerge when we evaluate our ability to explain the interindustry variance of technical efficiency by means of hypotheses resting on economic theory and past empirical evidence. Should no substantive model emerge that can offer a significant overall explanation of measured technical efficiency, we could not reject the hypothesis that technical efficiency has not been successfully measured.

7. This inference rests on the assumption that the size of the tail of observations removed by the data-editing rules declines with the average quality of data reported by the industry's establishments. We would defend this assumption on the basis of the conservatism of the data-editing procedures, chosen to minimize the risk of excluding a viable establishment that reported its data correctly. A large tail of establishments properly removed is then taken to suggest that a large population of poor-data establishments just barely escaped the knife, if reasonable continuity exists in the distribution of establishments' data-quality levels.

8. That conclusion may seem somewhat weakened by the fact that for production functions with gross output as the dependent variable, the rejection percentages do not differ between the NA and TI industries. On the other hand, that difference accords with the relatively even distribution of industries between the NA and TI categories obtained when the analysis is based on gross output.

9. For example, the correlation between $MMVA$ and λ is 0.385, significant at the 0.1 percent level.

10. See note 4 for details.

11. This demonstration makes no claim to get to the bottom of the problem, which would require a more sophisticated investigation of the foundations of the estimation procedure. Akio Torii reported (unpublished communication) a Monte Carlo study of the COLS estimation of the standard deviation of u, setting the true value at 1 and performing 5,000 trials for each of six sample sizes ranging from 10 to 500. He found that the estimated standard deviation is slightly biased upward and the efficiency measure EFF correspondingly biased downward when the number of observations is small. This result only deepens the mystery.

Chapter 5

1. A plant that uses more than the minimum quantities of all inputs, one might suspect, is likely as well as to make wrong decisions about their combinations or proportions. Indeed, one broadly based study (Shen 1973) did find evidence of a positive correlation among plants between technical inefficiency and the inefficient choice of factor proportions. Also see Viton (1986).

2. This could occur if capacity additions are determined noncooperatively and customers arrive randomly, seeking the quickest delivery at the collusive price.

3. See Williamson (1963); Crew, Jones-Lee, and Rowley (1971); Leibenstein (1976, chap. 12); McCain (1975).

4. See Worcester (1957), Brander and Spencer (1985), and Mankiw and Whinston (1986).

5. See Esposito and Esposito (1974); Caves, Jarrett, and Loucks (1979). A study of the consequences of abandoning restrictive agreements in British manufacturing industries reported the subsequent exit of substantial capacity, which (given that prices fell substantially and the quantity demanded accordingly increased) shows that the collusive agreements must have induced or sheltered considerable excess capacity (Swann et al. 1974).

6. Sources of data and information on the construction of variables are given in the appendix.

7. For evidence that terminating collusive agreements has increased productivity in U.S. manufacturing industries, see Erickson (1976).

8. A procedure frequently used has been to divide the concentration ratio by 1 plus the ratio of imports to domestic shipments. This procedure corrects the concentration ratio for the existence of sellers of competing imports who are by assumption not among the leading four sellers (taking domestic and foreign sellers together).

9. Bergsman (1974) inferred that tariff removal increases technical efficiency from the degree to which newly exposed import-competing producers sustain their outputs rather than contracting. It is not clear, however, that his method disentangles increased technical efficiency from lost quasi-rents.

10. Strong evidence for this proposition appears in studies of countries with smaller domestic markets and closer import competition than U.S. manufacturing industries typically faced in 1977 and before. See Bloch (1974) on Canada and Caves (1984) on Australia.

11. Førsund and Hjalmarsson (1987) studied this source of technical inefficiency in Scandinavian manufacturing industries. Also see Albach (1980) on the German chemical industry.

12. The same problem in predicting a causal influence on technical inefficiency may arise here as with product differentiation. While geographically fragmented markets should give rise to greater variance in productivity, it is not so clear that they would mainly augment the tail that indicates technical inefficiency. Geographic fragmentation would increase technical inefficiency if it gives rise to a collection of "large" or "favorable" markets in which "normal" productivity can be attained, accompanied by "small" or "unfavorable" ones in which lower productivity (not fully offset by higher unit prices) results.

13. As supporting evidence, Moomaw (1981) found that labor productivity varies significantly by region of the United States (after controlling for capital intensity, human capital, and urban location). This is consistent with dispersed levels of technical efficiency where production is dispersed regionally. It is also relevant that plant productivity increases with size of city, trading higher input and congestion costs against agglomeration advantages (Moomaw 1985); geographically dispersed industries are therefore likely to appear inefficient due to diverse urban densities.

14. The assumption is made (and supported by the data) that in most industries, externally controlled plants' sales are a minority of industry sales. The variable's mean is 34.7 percent, its standard deviation 15.9.

15. These data pertain to the year 1972, the latest available when the data base was organized. While an elaborate effort could be made to observe trends in institutional structures over the years preceding 1977 (when technical inefficiency is observed), the combination of weak theory and omnipresent data problems proved discouraging. Most measures of institutional patterns were taken as "levels" rather than "changes" and dated somewhere in the 1972–1977 period.

16. For comparison to *COVE*, *SPECE*'s mean is 30.2 and its standard deviation 15.3.

17. See Skinner (1974) for a managerial view of the problem and Caves (1975) and Schmenner (1980) for statistical evidence.

18. British evidence indicates that inefficiency is associated with horizontal multiplant operations; see Newbould (1970) and Cowling et al. (1980). The mean value of *MULT* is 11.6 percent, the standard deviation 11.1 percent.

19. Another basis for questioning the consistent efficiency of large companies is the insulation that their managers apparently have enjoyed from the threat of takeover in the market for corporate control. Managers of a larger firm could then indulge or tolerate greater inefficiency without fear of discipline by the market for corporate control. (This hypothesis makes more sense for 1977 than it would for the 1980s—the era of junk bonds.)

20. In a study of the productivity of British manufacturing industries, Davies and Caves (1987) found that low productivity was associated with a conjunction of divisive labor relations with managerial deficiencies in large-plant industries.

21. For examples, *Business Week*, June 6, 1986, pp. 100–114.

Chapter 6

1. To calculate the standard error of the technical-efficiency measure, one needs the sixth moment of the residuals from the underlying production function. We felt that noise would dominate the resulting calculation.

2. The absolute residuals from the regression show a strong negative association with this variable, *NOBS* (the square root of the number of observations in the underlying production-function calculation). Contrary to the usual textbook examples based on positive association, with this pattern the heteroskedasticity correction tends pervasively to increase our t-statistics. Usually the effect was to increase the significance of already significant variables; we shall identify instances in which a variable's significance depends on the correction.

3. Unless it is otherwise stated, equations reported in tables 6.1, 6.2, and 6.3 were estimated with the regressors *NOBS*, *SD(K/L)*, *RSIZE*, *PART*, and *R&D*, and each remained significant, with its coefficients relatively stable. We quote only the additional variables in these tables in order to avoid clutter.

4. Without the correction for heteroskedasticity, the coefficient of *VIOL*C3* is positive but not significant.

5. Recall that *VIOL* measures detected collusive arrangements, so that the hypothesis is compelled to rest on the assumption that detection reveals the efficiency-damaging effects of collusive arrangements without repairing them.

6. Theoretical research on industrial organization emphasizes that the correct way to specify the link between monopolistic distortions and concentration measures depends on the particular mode of competition assumed (Dansby and Willig 1979). However, research on competition and technical efficiency has not supplied any strong predictions about the form of the relationship or the appropriate way to measure concentration.

7. Imports could be matched to production data for a seemingly ample 278 of our industries, but when played against missing observations on other variables, the missing values of imports' share of domestic supply (*MS*) knocked down the number of industries available for estimation below 200.

8. In a study of the extent of exporting activity of different-sized plants in U.S. manufacturing industries, some indirect evidence suggested that technical inefficiency as measured by lambda increases with the coefficient of variation of the exports-shipments ratios of plants classified to an industry (Caves 1986). Presumably producing units that establish themselves successfully in export markets gain rents that on the evidence increase the (revenue) productivity of the most successful units and thus increase apparent technical inefficiency.

9. But it is not significant without the heteroskedasticity correction. Raising an industry's advertising-sales ratio by 5 percentage points is estimated to lower its reported efficiency by 0.08 standard deviation.

10. The significance of *RAD* depends on the White correction for heteroskedasticity. Notice that *RAD*'s presence in the model reduces considerably the size and significance of the coefficient of *DIV*. Increasing *RAD* by one standard deviation (374 miles) increases an industry's reported efficiency by only a very small amount, 0.016 standard deviation.

11. The greater size of *COVE*'s coefficient in low-R&D industries is not evident in all specifications—see equation 4—but the difference in significance never favors the high-R&D industries.

12. When *SPECE* is interacted in the same way, its coefficient is somewhat larger in high-R&D industries, and that for low-R&D industries is not statistically significant.

13. Without White's correction for heteroskedasticity, this negative effect is significant at 10 percent rather than 1 percent.

14. Lowering the sizes of the leading companies by one standard deviation (39 percent) has only a trivially small positive effect on technical efficiency.

15. This set of industries represents all that contain enough plants for the estimation of frontier production functions, not just the industries for which the technical-efficiency measure analyzed in this chapter could be obtained. See chapter 4.

16. The Spearman correlation between technical efficiency and the rejection count is in fact substantial, -0.41, but that is due to the high negative correlation between technical efficiency and the total number of plants retained after the deletions.

17. This conclusion should be considered uncertain because the negative effect of R&D on technical efficiency did not prove robust to changes in the dependent variable.

18. The absolute size of the largest firms in an industry (measured from their intraindustry activities only) appears to have a negative influence on efficiency, but the lack of strong hypothetical basis for this relation and the failure of a corollary to find support in chapter 7 cause us to downplay the result.

Chapter 7

1. The urgency of examining this question was increased by the empirical relationship (discussed in chapters 4 and 6) between efficiency and the number of observations used to estimate the frontier production functions. We concluded that the relation has a purely statistical foundation. But its possible implication that large-numbers markets are inefficient can be rejected more confidently if either the small-unit sectors of industries are not less efficient or their differential efficiency can be explained behaviorally.

2. Research on other countries such as Canada and Australia, where manufacturing industries have traditionally served small markets in competition with imports, tends to confirm the association between collusion and suboptimal scales due to an umbrella effect. See, for example, Baldwin and Gorecki (1985) and Caves (1984).

3. It is easy to rely on filtered data sources, such as records of publicly traded companies, in which the more profitable small enterprises are overrepresented. Such samples favor the conclusion that average profitability and size are negatively related. Studies of variations of profits with size within well-defined industries have found no significant relationship in most industries but considerable diversity that can be explained by means of the theory of entry and mobility barriers (Caves and Pugel 1980).

4. Casual data indicating the prevalence of such persons are not difficult to find. See *Wall Street Journal*, February 13, 1989, p. C1.

5. Table 7.1 is based on sets of industries for which the efficiency measures can be estimated for both the small- and large-plant sectors. The maximum number for small plants is 229, for large plants 235.

6. The influence of *EFFS* on *EFF* may account for one otherwise puzzling result in chapter 6. We found that efficiency decreases with the incidence of oligopolistic bargains but that maximum efficiency appears at the high end of what is considered the competitive range of concentration levels. We had no explanation why efficiency should decrease in more atomistic markets, although the problem of the "order statistics" phenomenon deterred us from probing the matter closely. Assume (as descriptive data indicate) that among industries, the absolute median size of establishments increases with seller concentration and decreases with the total number of establishments. Then any tendency for technical efficiency to decline in (very?) small establishments could account for chapter 6's nonlinear relationship.

7. The pattern of correlation coefficients for *EFF* based on gross output is similar, but all the correlations are lower (though still highly significant statistically). This is consistent with our previous finding that *EFF* based on gross output is a noisier measure than *EFF* based on value-added. The comparable regression of *EFF* based on gross output yields a 33 percent higher coefficient for *EFFS*; its $\bar{R}^2$ value is 0.57.

8. Most regressors proposed here were used previously in the analysis of *EFF*'s determinants and hence were described in chapter 5. Technical details of their sources and construction can be found in the appendix.

9. *MADS* is given preference because media advertising outlays involve greater minimum scales or thresholds than other types of sales promotion and thus should increase the diversity of beginners' levels of success.

10. *RSIZE* exhibits a correlation with *FEB*, the fraction of establishments employing twenty or more workers, 0.25, that is significant at 0.1 percent.

11. To check this assertion, we examined the correlation between *DIV* and *FEB*, the fraction of establishments employing twenty or more. It is 0.237, highly significant and consistent with the assertion.

12. As in the models reported in chapter 6, White's correction had the effect of reducing the estimated standard errors and thereby raising the *t*-statistics substantially because of the particular pattern of heteroskedasticity found in the data set. Some variables that are significant at 1 percent after the correction were significant at only 10 percent in its absence; we shall mention those cases in which significance depends on the correction.

13. Recall that in chapter 6 we found industries' efficiency overall to be negatively related to *PC1*.

14. The variable *GROW* is insignificant prior to application of the heteroskedasticity correction.

Chapter 8

1. These ideas can be found throughout writings of the Carnegie school, Leibenstein, Nelson and Winter, and others. Particularly relevant works are Cyert and George (1969), Bower (1970), and Nelson and Winter (1982, chap. 5).

2. While the possibility that competing business units differ in their efficiency levels (and hence in profitability and market share) has been importantly debated in industrial organization, there is surprisingly little evidence on the longevity of inefficient units or how long efficient units can sustain their advantages (or preserve them from replication by competitors). The assumption that organizational coalitions and the contract structures that bind them are sticky and not quickly reorganized seems plausible but cannot be readily documented.

3. This argument is related to the model originated by Scherer (1967) of the timing of innovation, which assumes diminishing returns to speeding the innovation process.

4. Peltzman (1977) demonstrated the correlation and asserted its cause to be the greater progressiveness of the firms that were increasing their market shares. But Scherer's (1979) reply cast doubt on the predominance of that causal explanation. The theoretical model of Nelson and Winter (1982, chap. 13) is particularly helpful for exposing the relation between innovation and resulting changes in the concentration of producers.

5. Recall Hayes and Wheelright (1984), quoted in chapter 1.

6. Empirical evidence relevant to the hypothesis is almost nonexistent. Nishimizu and Page (1982) did find an overall association between efficiency and productivity growth in Yugoslavia's industries. Davies and Caves (1987, chap. 6) found that the least efficient British industries in 1968 showed a weak tendency to improve their positions during 1968–1977; however, in that study, (static) efficiency was assessed not as technical efficiency but as the industry's average productivity shortfall from the U.S. counterpart industry, and productivity growth was also evaluated relative to the performance of the U.S. counterpart.

7. See table 6.5. This latter relationship is of marginal statistical significance.

8. Missing values are plugged with data from the National Science Foundation, a source that reports data for coarser industry classifications than the FTC but does cover the whole manufacturing sector.

9. Scherer (1982) obtained results that differed from one sample of productivity growth data to another but generally suggested that both influences are significant.

10. It should be noted that Lieberman's cross-section findings are based on the chemical-processing industries and might not apply to (say) industries with assembly-type technologies.

11. The same conclusion obtains if we think of the fixed factor as comprising heterogeneous units, with the lowest quality discarded as the industry contracts. Caves (1988) found some evidence that increased import competition tends to truncate the small-firm tails of U.S. manufacturing industries. If these contain the less-efficient firms in disproportionate numbers, as chapter 7 indicated, the hypothesis is supported.

12. *EFF* was entered in its natural units because the normality of the distributions of exogenous variables is not a matter of concern. We did ascertain that the results are essentially the same whether *EFF* is in natural units or its log-odds form. *EFFAJ* is, of course, based on the log-odds form.

13. We should note results for the alternative data set utilizing BLS data on productivity growth for a truncated (and nonrandom) subsample of industries. It shows no significant relation between *EFF* and *PR*, although the variable *R&D*, controlling for innovative opportunity, was a significant influence on *PR* (cf. Caves 1985). Clearly the BLS sample is the inferior one, with many fewer observations and a suspect pattern of deleted industries, to be stacked against only minor improvements in the measurement of *PR*. Yet this divergence between the $PR - EFF$ relations in the two samples reduces the confidence with which the null hypothesis on *EFF* is rejected for the ITA sample.

14. It is a victim of the heteroskedasticity correction, regularly significant at 10 percent (two-tail test) prior to this correction.

15. The correlation between ΔMS and ΔMSL is 0.35, indicating a fairly high degree of continuity in comparative-advantage changes over the period 1972–1986. For comparison, we calculated the correlation between changes for the same time periods in exports of the U.S. industries normalized by their total shipments and obtained -0.36. Stable trends in industries' levels of exposure to international trade cannot be taken for granted.

16. We could also calculate the correlation between *PR* in 1972–1977 and in 1977–1986 for 443 industries, nearly the whole set of four-digit industries in manufacturing. It is 0.095, lower than for the 222-industry sample but still significant at 5 percent.

17. In view of the large reduction of nonproduction worker overheads that apparently took place in the past decade, we wondered if *EFF* might be correlated with the 1977–1986 change in the ratio of production workers to total employees. No relation was found.

18. The most recent year available for the published data source, U.S. Bureau of the Census (1970, 1986). The match between the international trade and production classifications used in the United States is quite imperfect, as the former is based on commodities and the latter on the activities of production units. The majority of imperfections arise because the match pertains only to part of the commodities produced by the domestic industry (underinclusive) or to an aggregate of commodities larger than its output (overinclusive). These cases involve no necessary bias in the ratios of exports or imports to domestic activity. A smaller number involve biases (thought to be small) be-

cause the trade flow embraces a wider or narrower range of commodities than the production measure. Because we did not wish to lose observations from the relatively small eighty-eight-industry sample yielded by the data on technical efficiency and productivity growth, we were somewhat aggressive in forging these matches.

19. Measured as the difference between ratios for 1967 and 1982.

20. In an inventive mood, the interpreter could also see the negative correlation between the long-run (1967–1982) growth of import penetration and productivity growth at its outset (1967–1977) as the initial impact of unanticipated increases in import competition that first began to affect a number of major U.S. industries in the 1960s.

21. These correlations pertain to the 222-industry sample underlying table 8.1. For the maximum number of industries available (323), the correlations are a bit higher: 0.131 for 1977–1986 and 0.129 for 1972–1977, both significant at 2 percent. The mechanism by which increasing imports bestir adjustments that lead to increased exports has been assessed in an analysis of panel data pertaining to Canadian manufacturing industries (Caves 1989a).

Chapter 9

1. This conclusion is advanced cautiously because of our finding (chapter 4) that the efficiency levels indicated by stochastic frontier production functions decrease with the numbers of observations. We argued that it represents a purely statistical phenomenon ("order statistics") but recognize that a behavioral interpretation cannot be rejected out of hand.

2. We did find some evidence in chapter 6 that efficiency decreases with the absolute (intraindustry) sizes of an industry's largest firms, but a corollary of this relation failed to gain support in chapter 7. Nor did we find any effect of multiplant operation within industries on technical efficiency.

3. This concern has surfaced frequently, most recently in Jensen (1986). Evidence on Jensen's "free cash flow" hypothesis and managerial behavior in acquiring firms generally is reviewed by Caves (1989b).

4. Some progress has in fact been made along this line, with technical-efficiency measures calculated and reported for Australian industries (Harris 1987), calculated and analyzed (in Japanese) by Masu Uekusa and Akio Torii, and calculated but not yet analyzed by the National Economic Development Office in Great Britain.

References

Afriat, S. N. "Efficiency Estimation of Production Functions." *International Economic Review* 13 (October 1972), 568–98.

Aigner, D. J., and S. F. Chu. "On Estimating the Industry Production Function." *American Economic Review* 58 (September 1968), 826–39.

Aigner, D. J., C. A. K. Lovell, and P. Schmidt. "Formulation and Estimation of Stochastic Frontier Production Function Models." *Journal of Econometrics* 6 (July 1977), 21–37.

Albach, Horst. "Average and Best-Practice Production Functions in German Industry." *Journal of Industrial Economics* 29 (September 1980), 55–70.

Auquier, Antoine A. "Size of Firm, Exporting Behavior, and the Structure of French Industry." *Journal of Industrial Economics* 29 (December 1980), 203–18.

Bailey, Earl L. *Marketing-Cost Ratios of U.S. Manufacturers.* New York: Conference Board, 1975.

Bain, Joe S. *Barriers to New Competition.* Cambridge: Harvard University Press, 1956.

Bairam, Erkin I. "The Verdoorn Law, Returns to Scale and Industrial Growth: A Review of the Literature." *Australian Economic Papers* 26 (June 1987), 20–42.

Baldwin, John R., and Paul K. Gorecki. "The Determinants of Small Plant Market Share in Canadian Manufacturing Industries in the 1970s." *Review of Economics and Statistics* 67 (February 1985), 156–61.

Beeson, P., and S. Husted. "Patterns and Determinants of Productive Efficiency in State Manufacturing." *Journal of Regional Science* 29 (February 1989), 15–28.

Bergsman, Joel. "Commercial Policy, Allocative and 'X-Efficiency.'" *Quarterly Journal of Economics* 88 (August 1974), 409–33.

Berndt, Ernst R., and Laurits R. Christensen. "The Translog Function and the Substitution of Equipment, Structures, and Labor in U.S. Manufacturing, 1929–1968." *Journal of Econometrics* 1 (March 1973), 81–113.

Berndt, Ernst R., and Barry C. Field, eds. *Modeling and Measuring Natural Resource Substitution*. Cambridge: MIT Press, 1981.

Bloch, Harry. "Prices, Costs, and Profits in Canadian Manufacturing: The Influence of Tariffs and Concentration." *Canadian Journal of Economics* 7 (November 1974), 594–610.

Bower, Joseph L. *Managing the Resource Allocation Process*. Boston: Division of Research, Harvard Business School, 1970.

Bradburd, Ralph M., and A. Mead Over, Jr. "Organizational Costs, 'Sticky Equilibria,' and Critical Levels of Concentration." *Review of Economics and Statistics* 64 (February 1982), 50–58.

Brander, James A., and Barbara J. Spencer. "Tacit Collusion, Free Entry and Welfare." *Journal of Industrial Economics* 33 (March 1985), 277–94.

Bruning, Edward R., and Richard E. Olson. "The Use of Efficiency in the Testing for Scale Economies in the Motor Carrier Industry." *Journal of Transport Economics and Policy* 16 (September 1982), 277–94.

Burgess, David F. "Duality Theory and Pitfalls in the Specification of Technologies." *Journal of Econometrics* 3 (May 1975), 105–21.

Carlsson, Bo. "The Measurement of Efficiency in Production: An Application to Swedish Manufacturing Industries, 1968." *Swedish Journal of Economics* 74 (December 1972), 468–85.

Caves, Douglas W., Laurits R. Christensen, and Michael W. Tretheway. "U.S. Trunk Air Carriers, 1972–1977: A Multilateral Comparison of Total Factor Productivity." In *Productivity Measurement in Regulated Industries*, 47–76. Edited by T. G. Cowing and R. E. Stevenson. New York: Academic Press, 1981.

Caves, Richard E. "Export-led Growth: The Post-war Industrial Setting." In *Induction, Growth and Trade: Essays in Honor of Sir Roy Harrod*, 234–54. Edited by W. A. Eltis, M. FG. Scott, and J. N. Wolfe. Oxford: Clarendon Press, 1970.

Caves, Richard E. *Diversification, Foreign Investment, and Scale in North American Manufacturing Industries*. Ottawa: Economic Council of Canada, 1975.

Caves, Richard E. "Intraindustry Trade and Market Structure in the Industrial Countries." *Oxford Economic Papers* 33 (July 1981), 203–23.

Caves, Richard E. "Scale, Openness, and Productivity in Manufacturing." In *The Australian Economy: A View from the North*, 313–45. Edited by Richard E. Caves and Lawrence B. Krause. Washington, D.C.: Brookings Institution, 1984.

Caves, Richard E. "Interindustry Differences in Productivity Growth and Technical Efficiency." Harvard Institute of Economic Research, Discussion Paper No. 1130 (1985).

Caves, Richard E. "Exporting Behaviour and Market Structure: Evidence from the United States." In *Mainstreams in Industrial Organization* 1, 189–210.

Edited by H. W. de Jong and W. G. Shepherd. Dordrecht: Kluwer Academic, 1986.

Caves, Richard E. "Market Structure, Seller Competition, and Adjustment to International Disturbances." Presented at Conference on New Issues in Industrial Economics, Case Western Reserve University, Cleveland (1987).

Caves, Richard E. "Trade Exposure and Changing Structures of U.S. Manufacturing Industries." In *International Competitiveness*, 1–26. Edited by A. Michael Spence and Heather A. Hazard. Cambridge: Ballinger, 1988.

Caves, Richard E. "Trade Liberalization and Structural Adjustment in Canada: The Genesis of Intraindustry Trade." Harvard Institute of Economic Research, Discussion Paper No. 1427 (1989a).

Caves, Richard E. "Mergers, Takeovers, and Economic Efficiency: Foresight vs. Hindsight." *International Journal of Industrial Organization* 7 (March 1989b), 151–74.

Caves, Richard E., J. Peter Jarrett, and Michael K. Loucks. "Competitive Conditions and the Firm's Buffer Stocks: An Exploratory Analysis." *Review of Economics and Statistics* 61 (November 1979), 485–96.

Caves, Richard E., and Thomas A. Pugel. *Intraindustry Differences in Conduct and Performance: Viable Strategies in U.S. Manufacturing Industries.* Monograph Series in Finance and Economics No. 1980–2. New York: Graduate School of Business Administration, New York University, 1980.

Caves, Richard E., and Peter J. Williamson. "What Is Product Differentiation, Really?" *Joural of Industrial Economics* 34 (December 1985), 113–32.

Chen, Tain-jy, and De-piao Tang. "Comparing Technical Efficiency between Import-Substitution-Oriented Foreign Firms in a Developing Economy." *Journal of Development Economics* 26 (August 1987), 277–89.

Christensen, Laurits R., and William H. Greene. "Economies of Scale in U.S. Electric Power Generation." *Journal of Political Economy* 84 (August 1976), 655–76.

Clark, Kim B. "Unionization and Productivity: Micro-Econometric Evidence." *Quarterly Journal of Economics* 95 (December 1980), 613–40.

Corbo, Vittorio, and Jaime de Melo. "Technical Efficiency in a Highly Protected Economy: Preliminary Results for the Chilean Manufacturing Sector: 1967." Preliminary working paper, World Bank (1983).

Corbo, V., and P. Meller. "The Trans-Log Production Function: Some Evidence from Establishment Data." *Journal of Econometrics* 10 (June 1979), 193–99.

Cowing, T., D. Reifschneider, and R. Stevenson. "A Comparison of Alternative Frontier Cost Function Specifications." In *Developments in Econometric Analysis of Productivity*, chap. 4. Edited by Ali Dogramaci. Leiden: Kluwer-Nijhoff, 1983.

Cowling, Keith, Paul Stoneman, John Cubbin, John Cable, Graham Hall, Simon Domberger and Patricia Dutton. *Mergers and Economic Performance.* Cambridge: Cambridge University Press, 1980.

Crew, M. A., J. W. Jones-Lee, and C. K. Rowley. "X-Efficiency Theory versus Managerial Discretion Theory." *Southern Economic Journal* 38 (October 1971), 173–84.

Cyert, R. M., and K. D. George. "Competition, Growth, and Efficiency." *Economic Journal* 79 (March 1969), 23–41.

Dansby, Robert E., and Robert D. Willig. "Industry Performance Gradient Indexes." *American Economics Review* 69 (June 1979), 249–60.

Davies, Stephen, and Richard E. Caves. *Britain's Productivity Gap.* National Institute of Economic and Social Research, Occasional Paper No. 40. Cambridge: Cambridge University Press, 1987.

Davies, Stephen W., and Bruce R. Lyons. "Seller Concentration: The Technological Explanation and Demand Uncertainty." *Economic Journal* 92 (December 1982), 903–19.

Davis, Hiram S. "Relation of Capital-Output Ratio to Firm Size in American Manufacturing: Some Additional Evidence." *Review of Economics and Statistics* 38 (August 1956), 286–93.

Denny, Michael, and Melvin Fuss. "The Use of Approximation Analysis to Test for Separability and the Existence of Consistent Aggregates." *American Economic Review* 67 (June 1977), 404–18.

Downie, Jack. *The Competitive Process.* London: Gerald Duckworth & Co., 1958.

Erickson, W. Bruce. "Price Fixing Conspiracies: Their Long-Term Impact." *Journal of Industrial Economics* 24 (March 1976), 189–202.

Esposito, Frances Ferguson, and Louis Esposito. "Excess Capacity and Market Structure." *Review of Economics and Statistics* 56 (May 1974), 188–94.

Farrell, M. J. "The Measurement of Productive Efficiency." *Journal of the Royal Statistical Society* 120 (pt. 3, 1957), 253–82.

Fershtman, Chaim, and Eitan Muller. "Capital Investments and Price Agreements in Semicollusive Markets." *Rand Journal of Economics* 17 (Summer 1986), 214–26.

Flux, A. W. "Gleanings from the Census of Production Report." *Journal of the Royal Statistical Society* 76 (May 1913), 557–98.

Førsund, Finn R., and Lennart Hjalmarsson. "On the Measurement of Productive Efficiency." *Swedish Journal of Economics* 76 (June 1974), 141–54.

Førsund, Finn R., and Lennart Hjalmarsson. "Generalized Farrell Measures of Efficiency: An Application to Milk Processing in Swedish Dairy Plants." *Economic Journal* 89 (June 1979a), 294–315.

Førsund, Finn R., and Lennart Hjalmarsson. "Frontier Production Functions and Technical Progress: A Study of General Milk Processing in Swedish Dairy Plants." *Econometrica* 47 (July 1979b), 883–900.

Førsund, Finn R., and Lennart Hjalmarsson. *Analyses of Industrial Structure: A Putty-Clay Approach.* Stockholm: Industrial Institute for Economic and Social Research, 1987.

Førsund, Finn R., and Eilev S. Jansen. "On Estimating Average and Best Practice Production Functions via Cost Functions." *International Economic Review* 18 (June 1977), 463–76.

Førsund, Finn R., C. A. Knox Lovell, and Peter Schmidt. "A Survey of Frontier Production Functions and of Their Relationship to Efficiency Measurement." *Journal of Econometrics* 13 (May 1980), 5–25.

Frantz, Roger S. *X-Efficiency: Theory, Evidence and Applications.* Boston: Kluwer Academic, 1988.

Fraser, Donald R., and Peter S. Rose. "Bank Entry and Bank Performance." *Journal of Finance* 27 (March 1972), 65–78.

Freeman, Richard B., and James L. Medoff. *What Do Unions Do?* New York: Basic Books, 1984.

Greene, William H. "Maximum Likelihood Estimation of Econometric Frontier Functions." *Journal of Econometrics* 13 (May 1980), 27–56.

Griliches, Zvi. "Production Functions in Manufacturing: Some Additional Results." *Southern Economic Journal* 35 (October 1968), 151–56.

Griliches, Z., and V. Ringstad. *Economies of Scale and the Form of the Production Function: An Econometric Study of Norwegian Manufacturing Establishment Data.* Amsterdam: North-Holland Publishing Co., 1971.

Guth, Louis A. "Advertising and Market Structure Revisited." *Journal of Industrial Economics* 19 (April 1971), 179–98.

Harris, C. M. *Technical Efficiency of Australian Manufacturing.* Bureau of Industry Economics, Occasional Paper No. 4. Canberra: Bureau of Industry Economics, Department of Industry Technology and Commerce, 1987.

Harris, Richard. "Applied General Equilibrium Analysis of Small Open Economies with Scale Economies and Imperfect Competition." *American Economic Review* 74 (December 1984), 1016–32.

Hart, Oliver D. "The Market Mechanism as an Incentive Scheme." *Bell Journal of Economics* 14 (Autumn 1983), 366–82.

Hause, John C., and Gunnar Du Rietz. "Entry, Industry Growth, and the Microdynamics of Industry Supply." *Journal of Political Economy* 92 (August 1984), 733–57.

Hayes, Robert H., and Kim B. Clark. " Why Some Factories Are More Productive Than Others." *Harvard Business Review* 64 (September–October 1986), 66–73.

Hayes, Robert H., and Steven C. Wheelright. *Restoring Our Competitive Edge: Competing through Manufacturing*. New York: Wiley, 1984.

Hazledine, Tim. "The Possibility of Price Umbrellas in Canadian Manufacturing Industries." *International Journal of Industrial Organization* 2 (September 1984), 251–62.

Helpman, Elhanan. "International Trade in the Presence of Product Differentiation, Economies of Scale and Monopolistic Competition: A Chamberlin-Heckscher-Ohlin Approach." *Journal of International Economics* 11 (1981), 305–40.

Jensen, Michael C. "Agency Costs of Free Cash Flow, Corporate Finance, and Takeovers." *American Economic Review* 76 (May 1986), 323–29.

Johnston, J. *Econometric Methods*. 2d ed. New York: McGraw Hill, 1972.

Jondrow, James, C. A. Knox Lovell, Ivan S. Materov, and Peter Schmidt. "On the Estimation of Technical Inefficiency in the Stochastic Frontier Production Function." *Journal of Econometrics* 19 (August 1982), 233–38.

Jovanovic, Boyan. "Selection and the Evolution of Industry." *Econometrica* 50 (May 1982), 649–70.

Kaplan, Steven N. "Sources of Value in Management Buyouts." Ph.D. dissertation, Harvard University, 1988.

Katz, Harry C., Thomas A. Kochan, and Jeffrey H. Keefe. "Industrial Relations and Productivity in the U.S. Automobile Industry." *Brookings Papers on Economic Activity* 1987, no. 3, 685–715.

Kendall, M. G., and A. Stuart. *The Advanced Theory of Statistics*, vol. 1. New York: Hafner Publishing Co., 1969.

Kendrick, John M. *Postwar Productivity Trends in the United States, 1948–1969*. New York: National Bureau of Economic Research, 1973.

Klotz, Benjamin, Ray Madoo, and Reed Hansen. "A Study of High and Low Labor Productivity Establishments in U.S. Manufacturing." In *New Developments in Productivity Measurement and Analysis*, 239–86. Edited by John W. Kendrick and Beatrice N. Vaccara. Chicago: University of Chicago Press, 1981.

Kmenta, Jan. "On the Estimation of the CES Production Function." *International Economic Review* 8 (June 1967), 180–89.

Kopp, Raymond J. "The Measurement of Productive Efficiency: A Reconsideration." *Quarterly Journal of Economics* 96 (August 1981), 477–504.

Kopp, Raymond J., and V. Kerry Smith. "Frontier Production Function Estimates for Steam Electric Generation: A Comparative Analysis." *Southern Economic Journal* 47 (April 1980), 1049–59.

Krugman, Paul R. "Intraindustry Specialization and the Gains from Trade." *Journal of Political Economy* 89 (October 1981), 959–73.

Lawrence, Paul R., and Davis Dyer. *Renewing American Industry*. New York: Free Press, 1983.

Lecraw, Donald J. "Empirical Tests of X-Inefficiency: A Note." *Kyklos* 30, no. 1 (1977), 116–20.

Lee, Lung-fei, and William G. Tyler. "The Stochastic Frontier Production Function and Average Efficiency: An Empirical Analysis." *Journal of Econometrics* 7 (June 1978), 385–89.

Leibenstein, Harvey. "Allocative Efficiency vs. 'X-Efficiency.'" *American Economic Review* 56 (June 1966), 392–415.

Leibenstein, Harvey. "Competition and X-Efficiency: Reply." *Journal of Political Economy* 81 (May 1973), 763–77.

Leibenstein, Harvey. *Beyond Economic Man: A New Foundation for Microeconomics*. Cambridge. Harvard University Press, 1976.

Lemelin, Andre. "Relatedness in the Patterns of Interindustry Diversification." *Review of Economics and Statistics* 64 (November 1982), 646–57.

Lieberman, Marvin B. "The Learning Curve and Pricing in the Chemical Processing Industries." *Rand Journal of Economics* 15 (Summer 1984), 213–28.

Lippman, S. A., and R. P. Rumelt. "Uncertain Imitability: An Analysis of Interfirm Differences in Efficiency under Competition." *Bell Journal of Economics* 13 (Autumn 1982), 418–38.

McCain, Roger A. "Competition, Information, Redundancy: X-Efficiency and the Cybernetics of the Firm." *Kyklos* 28, no. 2 (1975), 286–308.

MacDonald, James M. "R&D and the Directions of Diversification." *Review of Economics and Statistics* 67 (November 1985), 583–90.

Mairesse, Jacques, and Zvi Griliches. "Heterogeneity in Panel Data: Are There Stable Production Functions?" National Bureau of Economic Research, Working Paper No. 2619 (1988).

Mankiw, N. Gregory, and Michael D. Whinston. "Free Entry and Social Inefficiency." *Rand Journal of Economics* 17 (Spring 1986), 48–58.

Mansfield, Edwin. "Entry, Gibrat's Law, Innovation, and the Growth of Firms." *American Economic Review* 52 (December 1962), 1023–51.

Meeusen, Wim, and Julien van den Broeck. "Efficiency Estimation of Cobb-Douglas Production Functions with Composed Error." *International Economic Review* 18 (June 1977a), 435–44.

Meeusen, Wim, and Julien van den Broeck. "Technical Efficiency and Dimensions of the Firm: Some Results on the Use of Frontier Production Functions." *Empirical Economics* 2, no. 2 (1977b), 109–22.

Meller, Patricio. "Allocative Frontiers for Industrial Establishments of Different Sizes." *Explorations in Economic Research* 3 (Summer 1976), 379–407.

Mellow, Wesley. "Employer Size and Wages." *Review of Economics and Statistics* 64 (August 1982), 495–501.

Moomaw, Ronald L. "Production Efficiency and Region." *Southern Economic Review* 48 (October 1981), 344–57.

Moomaw, Ronald L. "Firm Location and City Size: Reduced Productivity Advantages as a Factor in the Decline of Manufacturing in Urban Areas." *Journal of Urban Economics* 17 (January 1985), 73–89.

Mueller, Dennis C. "Mergers and Market Share." *Review of Economics and Statistics* 47 (May 1985), 259–67.

Müller, Jürgen. "On Sources of Measured Technical Efficiency: The Impact of Information." *American Journal of Agricultural Economics* 56 (November 1974), 730–38.

Nelson, Richard R., and Sidney G. Winter. *An Evolutionary Theory of Economic Change*. Cambridge: Harvard University Press, 1982.

Newbould, Gerald D. *Management and Merger Activity*. Liverpool: Guthstead, 1970.

Nishimizu, Mieko, and John M. Page, Jr. "Total Factor Productivity Growth, Technological Progress, and Technical Efficiency Change: Dimensions of Productivity Change in Yugoslavia, 1965–78." *Economic Journal* 92 (December 1982), 920–38.

Olson, Jerome A., Peter Schmidt, and Donald M. Waldman. "A Monte Carlo Study of Estimators of Stochastic Frontier Production Functions." *Journal of Econometrics* 13 (May 1980), 67–82.

Olson, Mancur. *The Rise and Decline of Nations: Economic Growth, Stagflation, and Social Rigidities*. New Haven: Yale University Press, 1982.

Owen, Donald B. *Handbook of Statistical Tables*. Reading, MA: Addison-Wesley, 1962.

Page, John M., Jr. "Technical Efficiency and Economic Performance: Some Evidence from Ghana." *Oxford Economic Papers* 32 (July 1980), 319–39.

Pashigian, Peter. "The Effect of Market Size on Concentration." *International Economic Review* 10 (October 1969), 291–314.

Peltzman, Sam. "The Gains and Losses from Industrial Concentration." *Journal of Law and Economics* 20 (October 1977), 229–63.

Pitt, Mark M., and Lung-fei Lee. "The Measurement and Sources of Technical Inefficiency in the Indonesian Weaving Industry." *Journal of Development Economics* 9 (August 1981), 43–64.

Porter, Michael E. "The Structures within Industries and Companies' Performance." *Review of Economics and Statistics* 71 (May 1979), 214–27.

Ravenscraft, David J., and F. M. Scherer. *Mergers, Sell-offs, and Economic Efficiency*. Washington, D.C.: Brookings Institution, 1987.

Richmond, J. "Estimating the Efficiency of Production." *International Economic Review* 15 (June 1974), 515–21.

Ringstad, Vidar. "Economies of Scale and the Form of the Production Function: Some New Estimates." *Scandinavian Journal of Economics* 80, no. 3 (1978), 251–64.

Samuels, J. M., and D. J. Smyth. "Profits, Variability of Profits, and Firm Size." *Economica* 35 (May 1968), 127–39.

Saxonhouse, Gary R. "Estimated Parameters as Dependent Variables." *American Economic Review* 66 (March 1976), 178–83.

Scharfstein, David. "Product-Market Competition and Managerial Slack." *Rand Journal of Economics* 19 (Spring 1988), 147–55.

Scherer, F. M. "Firm Size, Market Structure, Opportunity and the Output and Patented Inventions." *American Economic Review* 55 (December 1965), 1097–1123.

Scherer, F. M. "Research and Development Resource Allocation under Rivalry." *Quarterly Journal of Economics* 81 (August 1967), 359–94.

Scherer, F. M. "The Determinants of Industrial Plant Sizes in Six Nations." *Review of Economics and Statistics* 55 (May 1973), 135–45.

Scherer, F. M. "Industrial Structure, Scale Economies, and Worker Alienation." In *Essays on Industrial Organization in Honor of Joe S. Bain*, 105–21. Edited by R. T. Masson and P. D. Qualls. Cambridge. Ballinger, 1976.

Scherer, F. M. "The Causes and Consequences of Rising Industrial Concentration: A Comment." *Journal of Law and Economics* 22 (April 1979), 191–208.

Scherer, F. M. "Interindustry Technology Flows and Productivity Growth." *Review of Economics and Statistics* 64 (November 1982), 627–34.

Scherer, F. M., et al. *The Economics of Multi-Plant Operation: An International Comparisons Study*. Cambridge: Harvard University Press, 1975.

Schmenner, Roger W. "Choosing New Industrial Capacity: On-Site Expansion, Branching, and Relocation." *Quarterly Journal of Economics* 95 (August 1980), 103–19.

Schmidt, Peter. "On the Statistical Estimation of Parametric Frontier Production Functions." *Review of Economics and Statistics* 58 (May 1976), 238–39.

Schmidt, Peter. "Frontier Production Functions." *Econometric Reviews* 4, no. 2 (1985–1986), 289–328.

Schmidt, Peter, and C. A. Knox Lovell. "Estimating Technical and Allocative Inefficiency Relative to Stochastic Production and Cost Frontiers." *Journal of Econometrics* 9 (February 1979), 343–66.

Schmidt, Peter, and C. A. Knox Lovell. "Estimating Stochastic Production and Cost Frontiers When Technical and Allocative Inefficiency Are Correlated." *Journal of Econometrics* 13 (May 1980), 83–100.

Seitz, Wesley D. "Productive Efficiency in the Steam-Electric Generating Industry." *Journal of Political Economy* 79 (July–August 1971), 878–86.

Shapiro, Kenneth H., and Jürgen Müller. "Sources of Technical Efficiency: The Roles of Modernization and Information." *Economic Development and Cultural Change* 25 (January 1977), 293–310.

Shen, T. Y. "Economies of Scale, Expansion Path, and Growth of Plants." *Review of Economics and Statistics* 47 (November 1965), 420–28.

Shen, T. Y. "Competition, Technology and Market Shares." *Review of Economics and Statistics* 50 (February 1968), 293–310.

Shen, T. Y. "Economies of Scale, Penrose Effect, Growth of Plants and Their Size Distribution." *Journal of Political Economy* 78 (July–August, 1970), 702–16.

Shen, T. Y. "Technology Diffusion, Substitution, and X-Efficiency." *Econometrica* 41 (March 1973), 263–84.

Sherman, Howard J. *Profits in the United States: An Introduction to a Study of Economic Concentration and Business Cycles.* Ithaca: Cornell University Press, 1968.

Siegfried, John, George Sweeney, and Katherine Maddox. "The Incidence of Monopoly Profits in Consumer Goods Industries." In U.S. Federal Trade Commission, *The Economics of Firm Size, Market Structure and Social Performance.* Edited by John J. Siegfried. Washington, D.C.: Government Printing Office, 1980.

Skinner, Wickham. "The Decline, Fall, and Renewal of Manufacturing Plants." *Industrial Engineering* (October 1974), pp. 32–38.

Stevenson, Rodney E. "Likelihood Functions for Generalized Stochastic Frontier Estimation." *Journal of Econometrics* 13 (May 1980), 57–66.

Stigler, George J. *Capital and Rates of Return in Manufacturing Industries.* Princeton, N.J.: Princeton University Press, 1963.

Stigler, George J. "The Xistence of X-Efficiency." *American Economic Review* 66 (May 1976), 213–16.

Stonebraker, Robert J. "Corporate Profits and the Risk of Entry." *Review of Economics and Statistics* 58 (February 1976), 33–39.

Summa, Timo. *Development of Intra-Industrial Efficiency: An Application of the Frontier and Short-run Production Functions Based on Micro-Data.* Series C 36. Helsinki: Research Institute of the Finnish Economy, 1985.

Swann, Dennis, et al. *Competition in British Industry: Restrictive Practices Legislation in Theory and Practice.* London: Allen & Unwin, 1974.

Terleckyj, Nestor. *Effects of R&D on the Productivity Growth of Industries.* Washington, D.C.: National Planning Association, 1974.

Timmer, C. Peter. "Using a Probabilistic Frontier Production Function to Measure Technical Inefficiency." *Journal of Political Economy* 79 (July–August 1971), 775–95.

Todd, Douglas. *The Relative Efficiency of Small and Large Firms.* Committee of Inquiry on Small Firms, Research Report No. 18. London: Her Majesty's Stationery Office, 1971.

Tyler, William G. "Technical Efficiency in Production in a Developing Country: An Empirical Examination of the Brazilian Plastics and Steel Industries." *Oxford Economic Papers* 31 (November 1979), 477–95.

Tyler, William G., and Lung-fei Lee. "On Estimating Stochastic Frontier Production Functions and Average Efficiency: An Empirical Analysis with Colombian Micro Data." *Review of Economics and Statistics* 61 (August 1979), 436–38.

U.S. Bureau of the Census. *U.S. Commodity Exports and Imports as Related to Output, 1967 and 1966.* Series E52, No. 10. Washington, D.C.: Government Printing Office, 1970.

U.S. Bureau of the Census. *U.S. Commodity Exports and Imports and Related to Output, 1982 and 1981.* Series E52–18. Washington, D.C.: Government Printing Office, 1986.

U.S. Bureau of Labor Statistics. *Time Series Data for Input-Output Industries.* Bulletin No. 2018. Washington, D.C.: Government Printing Office, 1979.

U.S. Bureau of Labor Statistics. *Productivity Measures for Selected Industries, 1958–84.* Bulletin No. 2256. Washington, D.C.: Government Printing Office, 1986.

Viton, Philip A. "The Question of Efficiency in Urban Bus Transportation." *Journal of Regional Science* 26 (August 1986), 499–513.

Waldman, Donald M. "Properties of Technical Efficiency Estimators in the Stochastic Frontier Model." *Journal of Econometrics* 25 (July 1984), 353–64.

Weiss, Leonard W. "Survival Technique and the Extent of Suboptimal Capacity." *Journal of Political Economy* 72 (June 1964), 246–61.

Weiss, Leonard W., and George A. Pascoe, Jr. *Adjusted Concentration Ratios in Manufacturing, 1972 and 1977.* Statistical Report of the Bureau of Economics to the Federal Trade Commission. Washington, D.C.: Federal Trade Commission, 1986.

White, Halbert. "A Heteroskedasticity-Consistent Covariance Matrix Estimator and a Direct Test for Heteroskedasticity." *Econometrica* 48 (May 1980), 817–38.

White, Lawrence J. "The Determinants of the Relative Importance of Small Business." *Review of Economics and Statistics* 64 (February 1982), 42–49.

Williamson, Oliver E. "Managerial Discretion and Business Behavior." *American Economic Review* 53 (December 1963), 1033–57.

Williamson, Oliver E. "Hierarchical Control and Optimum Firm Size." *Journal of Political Economy* 75 (April 1967), 123–38.

Williamson, Oliver E. "Economies as an Antitrust Defense: The Welfare Tradeoffs." *American Economic Review* 58 (March 1968), 18–36.

Wilson, George W., and Joseph M. Jadlow. "Competition, Profit Incentives, and Technical Efficiency in the Provision of Nuclear Medicine Services." *Bell Journal of Economics* 13 (Autumn 1982), 472–82.

Winter, Sidney G. "Satisficing, Selection, and the Innovating Remnant." *Quarterly Journal of Economics* 85 (May 1971), 237–61.

Worcester, D. A. "Why 'Dominant Firms' Decline." *Journal of Political Economy* 65 (August 1957), 338–46.

Yotopoulos, P. A., and L. J. Lau. "A Test for Relative Economic Efficiency." *American Economic Review* 63 (March 1973), 214–23.

Zellner, A., J. Kmenta, and J. Dreze. "Specification and Estimation of Cobb-Douglas Production Function Models." *Econometrica* 34 (October 1966), 784–95.

Index